I0018608

LEARNING DATA STRUCTURES IN THE GENERATIVE AI ERA

Dinesh C. Verma

Copyright © 2025 Dinesh C. Verma

All rights reserved.

DEDICATION

Dedicated to my loving wife Paridhi and my wonderful children - Archit and Riya, who have always encouraged me to write books and share knowledge with others.

TABLE OF CONTENTS

Introduction

The idea for writing this book came at the end of the semester when I taught a course on data structure at St. John's University in Queens as an adjunct in Fall 2024. Generative AI and code Large Language Models were becoming mainstream at the time and there were several debates and conflicting opinions around permitting students to use them for coursework.

As I started interacting with the students during the semester long course, I realized the futility of asking students not to use GenAI tools available to them. I had no effective way to detect or prevent any student from using any services available on the Internet. Even if I could detect such usage to prevent it, the right thing in education is to teach students how to use new tools, not forbid them from using them.

When students used GenAI services, it was obvious to me that the existing data structure textbooks I was using were largely obsoleted by GenAI. Most of the practice problems and example in the textbooks were already part of the training corpus of the AI models, and anyone could generate code in seconds for most of the interesting classical computer science problems. Furthermore, large portions of textbooks that dealt with implanting lists, trees and hash-tables seemed superfluous in the presence of extensive collections libraries and GenAI code generation.

I decided to revamp my instruction to focus on abstractions – teaching students to think how to define and use abstractions – utilizing the GenAI tools to generate code that implements those abstractions. As a general concept, abstraction has been an essential part of computer science but generally overshadowed by the task of programming. With GenAI tools, the focus shifts to defining abstractions rather than coding them up. Another key deliberate difference in this book is the lack of references for students to dig deeper into topics they choose. That search for references is a good use of GenAI tools and it is better for students to learn how to find current updated references than to follow a static set of references.

The final chapter of this book contains some software program that the students can develop to show that they have mastered the art of defining abstractions and using data structures to implement the software programs. This approach should help drive their critical thinking approach since the traditional approach of testing specific problems at end of each chapter faces the challenge that most traditional specific problems in data structures are answered readily by current GenAI tools.

This book is developed as an aide to teach students to understand data structures and to use them to solve interesting problems. While I have tried to avoid mistakes, it likely contains some and would need improvements as I get additional student feedback.

The code corresponding to the problems in this book can be seen at the URL: https://github.com/dinesh-personal/data_structures/

PART I: The Basics

In this part of the book, we cover some of the fundamental skills needed to learn about data structures and analyze the algorithms that we will cover in the book. Since data structures are taught relatively early in Computer Science, some of the students may not be familiar with these concepts. Even for those who have learnt the concept in one of the prerequisite courses, a quick refresher is useful.

The first chapter in this part provides an overview of the approach taken in this book, and the philosophical approach for why this type of book is made necessary by the rise of GenAI.

The second chapter introduces some of the common mathematical principles that a student of data structure must know – including the concept of propositional logic, mathematical induction, approaches for summing up sequences, and proof by contradiction.

The third chapter in this part covers an overview of the approaches used for analyzing the performance of algorithms. We will be using the approaches described in this section for the analysis of various operations on different data structures covered in subsequent sections.

The fourth chapter in this section defines the concept of an abstraction, and how data structures are abstractions related to information and data. It also clarifies the difference between data and data structures. A focus on abstractions, as opposed to implementation of data structure implementation, is the primary shift in instruction of data structure that is made necessary by the rise of Generative AI.

Chapter 1.   Philosophy Behind this Book

There have been many excellent books written about data structures and algorithms in many different programming languages, and they have been used successfully for the instruction of the topics to computer science students in their undergraduate curriculum. A natural question that arises is the need for yet another book on data structures when so many excellent ones already exist.

When I was charged with teaching data structures to an undergraduate class at St. John's University, I was faced with the challenge of selecting a good textbook for instruction. I scoured through all the available textbooks and found several excellent ones, except all of them were written before the advent of Generative AI (GenAI). As a result, they focused primarily on aspects of data structures that were rendered superfluous with the advent of GenAI tools.

To draw an analogy, their focus was on teaching methods for long division when the students already have access to a powerful calculator to perform any division in the matter of few minutes by typing in the requisite numbers. While nobody can argue with the benefits of learning long division, it has not been the primary focus for arithmetic instruction since the advent of computers.

GenAI enables us to generate a functioning program by specifying prompts in natural language. While the technology is far from perfect (and one can argue that it is over-hyped), it does have a significant impact on the instruction and learning of computer science.

In this book, I have attempted to create instructional material for data structures which leverage the capabilities of GenAI tools and enable the student to learn about the properties of the structures, and using the data structures to solve interesting problems -- rather than details on approaches to implement the data structures. I hope this book will be useful to anyone who wants to learn about data structures while leveraging the full power of GenAI tools.

In the introductory chapter of this book, it is pertinent that we take a high-level look at GenAI, what the technology is capable of, and also what the technology is not capable of.

Overview of Generative AI

GenAI is technology that allows the generation of a new content in response to a prompt. The generation is done by means of an AI model that has been trained on a large corpus of data. While the exact details of the structure of these models is beyond the scope of this book (See Reference [1] for a broad review), it would suffice to say that these models are trained on a very large corpus of data, and learn the patterns underlying the corpus of training data – in essence learning with a high probability what sequences are likely to follow the sequences of characters included in the prompt.

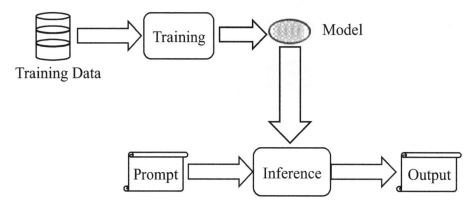

Figure 1. Generic Process for AI models

The general process of training and using an AI model is shown in Figure 1. An AI model is trained using training data which for most GenAI covers a large set of data collected from various sources on the Internet. The fully trained model is used for inference, which generally takes an input from the user, traditionally called a prompt for large language models, and generates an output sequence of text. The output sequence may consist of a program or a new piece of text.

The training data sources may include samples of code that are available in public software repositories, as well as samples from course books that are available in the public domain. The training process is based on approaches that use the training data to predict the next word occurring in a sequence, or similar tasks where both the input prompt and the corresponding output can be easily determined from the training data. The model learns the likelihood of various outputs occurring on a combination of the input sequences and uses that to generate the output as needed. With most types of GenAI models, the inference can produce output that is new – in the sense that it need not be present in the training data set. At the same time, the output is determined based on the probability of how likely an output text is given the prompt and statistically like the types of prompts and outputs that are present in the training data.

The training process requires significant resources to examine all the training data that needs to be processed, and is much slower compared to the inference process, which can generate the output for a prompt in a relatively short amount of time. Many companies offer pretrained models that can perform a variety of tasks, others provide online services that will take a prompt and generate the desired output.

From the perspective of a student of computer science, one need not spend an infinite amount of time sitting down and programming a task. Suppose one runs across this problem which is a staple in introductory physics classes and provides a simple example for introductory programming:

```
Write a program in Java which computes the velocity of an
object dropped from a tower of height 100 feet when that object
reaches ground.
```

4

For anyone learning Java (or any other programming language) writing this program can take a significant amount of time. However, one can use any among a myriad of AI based services available on the Internet and ask it the same question, and the service will immediately output the software program – sometimes with a helpful explanatory note as well.

```
public class VelocityCalculator {
    public static void main(String[] args) {
      double height = 100; // height in feet
      double gravity = 32.2; //acceleration due to gravity in ft/s^2
      double velocity = Math.sqrt(2 * gravity * height);
      System.out.println("Velocity at ground:"+velocity+ " ft/s.");
    }
}
```

While the exact code output may vary depending on the service used, most of the GenAI services do an incredible job at understanding that the unit is in feet, using the right acceleration units for gravity, as well as computing and printing the right value.

While this is an amazing capability that is widely available, the technology does have some significant limitations. The GenAI based services work well when prompted to generate programs that are common, available at multiple sites on Internet, and therefore likely to be included in their training data. Equations for calculating velocity due to gravity are found in multiple textbooks and programs to calculate these equations published in various textbooks and online sources – all of which can be expected to be a part of the training data for the AI model. GenAI does a great job in providing solutions to problems similar to ones present in their training corpus, but they generally do not do a great job at handling prompts or situations that is very different than the ones in the training data. If one were to ask those services to generate a program to calculate the position of the Sun according to the principles of *Surya Siddhanta by Aryabhatta* – an ancient Sanskrit text from India which is unlikely to be in the corpus of any of the common GenAI services, they are unlikely to generate a good software for that. Or at the very least, my attempts at prompting many of the popular GenAI services at this task failed when attempted in November of 2024.

Despite their limitations, the capability of GenAI poses a challenge for most instructors and students of computer science introductory courses. Computer science is a field that is more than half a century old (assuming we consider it starting around 1960), and over these years, many textbooks have addressed the common problems and various solutions to these problems. For the student learning the basics, it is too much of a temptation to use these services to solve the problems that can be found in the usual textbooks. For the instructor, the traditional and time-tested problems are now trivial to solve and creating new assignments and new problems become a challenge. The only viable option for an instructor is to adopt this new technology and teach students the best way to leverage the technology.

The higher objective for which students are enrolling for courses in data structures is to strengthen their ability to develop software and to become better software engineers. As instructors, it means that we need to move away from teaching students how to implement existing data structures and instead focus on teaching them how to leverage data structures, how to decide which data structures to use, and how to best solve problems using their knowledge of data structures.

In this book, we take an abstraction-oriented approach to learn about data structures and how they can be used.

A Philosophical Diversion

This section may be considered a diversion by some, but it is a justification for the philosophy behind this book. The change that is being caused by GenAI is not an unseen phenomenon. The approach for instruction needs to change every time a new technology innovation changes the way society manages knowledge. Such technological innovations have happened continuously from the era of our prehistoric hunter and gatherer ancestors.

In the age where our ancestors lived a hunter-gatherer existence, people lived in small groups. In such groups, it was important to pass information about where a supply of water may be found, which type of fruits and berries were safe to gather and eat, which ones were unsafe, and where one should go to hunt deer or other animals to get a supply of meat. The teachers would typically be the older members in the group, who may know the terrain better but not be as agile as the younger members in the group. As the teachers pass on the useful information to the younger students, they would have to rely on the techniques such as memory and repetition to make sure that the information is being relayed properly.

This hunter gatherer society likely foraged for food in the warm summer months and sheltered in a cave during the cold winter months. The winter months were ideal for the older members of the community to pass the knowledge about the land and its characteristics to the younger members. Without the technology of writing, the society would have pass knowledge through oral communication and memorization. In that society, we can envision a teacher (i.e. the older member) and the student (the younger member) interacting to pass the tribal knowledge down during the long winter months. The teacher would teach the student about the best path to take from the cave to the fruit-bearing trees in spring. If the teacher survived the winter, he or she may be able to show the path in person. But given the short life-expectancy and the prevalence of dangerous predators, there would be no guarantee that the teacher will be around to show the path next summer, and it was best for the family group to ensure that the young ones learned about the path sooner rather than later. The teacher would describe the path that ought to be followed and ask the student to repeat it to check if there are any mistakes. The student would likely repeat it multiple times without mistake to make sure that the paths had been memorized properly.

Humanity has always been innovative and when summer came around, the teacher and student emerged from the cave, they might have encountered another family group which had made a great technological breakthrough for the times. They discovered a method to create marks on stones and cave walls. The great innovation, the ability to make cave paintings, would transform the entire teaching method. Memorization and repetition by rote would no longer be that important. The ability to make marks on the cave and the ability to read those marks would have become the more desirable skill. In other words, the invention of cave painting would have caused a whole transformation of the method by which knowledge got passed down. Maps and marks on landmarks would be used as the method of instruction, instead of a reliance on memorization.

While the key skill needed to solve the problem would have changed from memorization to mark-creation and mark-reading, the important problem to be solved remained the same – find the safest and best approach to go from place A to place B.

Other technology innovations would occur in the primitive society. People would learn the technology to make symbols and write down things on palm-leaves, papyrus leaves, baked clay tablets or similar persistent material. Reading and writing would be the key skills to learn, perhaps overshadowing the previous skills of map-reading and memorization. If one had to go from place A to place B, one needed to learn the art of reading and writing, instead of interpreting the marks on the landmarks.

As the march for technology innovation continued, printing presses would be invented, forcing the instruction approach to undergo another transformation. The large number of books would be stored within libraries, and it would become important to be able to find the relevant books that provided information relevant to go from a place A to a place B. While the nature of places that one needed to go would have changed in societies that maintain libraries (e.g. people may be going to the King's ballroom dance instead of the trees with edible fruits), the basic problem would still be going from one place to another.

If teachers insisted on maintaining the old method of instruction as the only way to learn how to go from one place to another, students would not be learning the best skills suitable for their social context. Instruction needs to evolve with the times to adjust to technical innovation. Approaches that try to ban technical innovation to preserve the instruction method are neither desirable nor necessary for the improvement of society.

Another example of technology innovation disrupting instruction method is more recent, namely the invention of the calculator. When calculations needed to be done by hand, it was important to learn techniques such as long division. These techniques, while tedious, were invaluable skills for engineers and scientists. But when the calculator was invented, instruction of long division also became less important, and students focused on the best way to use the calculator to solve problem, as opposed to mastering the art of long division.

GenAI is neither the first nor the last technology innovation that will require an adjustment in the methods of instruction. We need to adopt our method of instruction so that the GenAI systems are used to assist in the main task of learning computer science, not ban it in an attempt to preserve the current approach for instruction. Our goal is to assist our students become better at solving their primary problem, not in holding on to an old approach for instruction.

Just like the primary problem to be solved for our hunter and gatherer ancestors was to safely go from place A to place B, we need to ask ourselves what is the primary problem that our students need to solve today. For any student of computer science, the primary problem likely is developing software systems which solve problems considered important to business and society. We need to teach students how to rapidly develop software using all tools available at their disposal.

Coming to the subject of data structures, it means that we need to teach the students how to best use data structures to solve problems they may encounter in practice. GenAI has made the task of implementing standard types of data structures very easy. Traditional data structure books which focus on the algorithms for internal implementation of arrays, queues, lists and trees may not be that relevant today since GenAI can easily generate the code for these algorithms in many programming languages. In light of this fact, instruction of data structure must focus on how those data structures can be used to solve various problems, instead of internal implementations of the data structure.

Chapter Summary/Key Takeaways

This chapter provides the brief justification for writing a new book on the instruction of data structures. The key ideas covered in this chapter are:

- GenAI requires that data structures (and other topics in Computer Science) be taught in a different manner

- The focus of instruction should not be on the implementation of data structures but on their use-cases

- The focus of instruction must move to a higher level of problem solving than just coding up data structures

In the next chapter, we will cover some basic mathematical principles that everyone learning about data structures should be familiar with.

Chapter 2.   Common Mathematical Principles

A chapter on common mathematical principles is generally not included in traditional book on data structures. However, during my instruction experience, I realized that not every student coming into the class has the same background in mathematics. As a result, it is useful to summarize some of basic concepts and principles of mathematics that are useful for computer science and learning of data structures in this introductory chapter.

The goal of this chapter is not to go deep into mathematical principles or cover all the mathematical principals comprehensively. Those who want to have a more rigorous treatment may want to refer to other books [1] [2].

Propositional Logic

As we learn about data structures and using them to solve various problems, we would like to be able to prove some properties about them. In order to prove any property, the general approach is to start from a set of propositions that are generally accepted as true and use a series of well-reasoned steps to derive the proof of the property. We will follow the basic concepts of propositional logic. A more rigorous and detailed overview of logic can be found on other books [2].

We will assume that a statement that is made can only possibly be true or false. There are no half-truths or half-falsehoods. Other equivalent names for statements are predicates, propositions or assertions. There are some statements that we implicitly assume to be true. Those statements are called axioms.

Statements can be combined to make other statements. The common types of combinations that can be made for statements are conjunction, disjunction and implication. For example, one can make the following two statements (or assertions/predicates/propositions):

1. This program will finish in a time proportional to the number of inputs

2. This program will use memory proportional to the number of inputs

Either of the two statements can be true or false. The combinations of these two statements would be the following statements:

- *Conjunction*: This program will finish in a time proportional to the number of inputs, and this program will use memory proportional to the number of inputs.

- *Disjunction*: Either this program will finish in a time proportional to the number of inputs, or this program will use memory proportional to the number of inputs.

- *Implication*: If this program will finish in a time proportional to the number of inputs, then this program will use memory proportional to the number of inputs.

- *Exclusive Or*: Exactly one of these two will happen - Either this program will finish in a time proportional to the number of inputs, or this program will use memory proportional to the number of inputs.

- *Equivalence*: This program will finish in a time proportional to the number of inputs, if and only if this program will use memory proportional to the number of inputs.

The combined statements will be true or false depending on whether the original statements were true or false. A conjunction is true only if both statements in it are true. A disjunction is true if any one of the statements in it is true. An implication is true when the statement after the 'then' part is true whenever the sentence before the 'then' part is true. An exclusive or (often abbreviated as XOR) is true only if exactly one of the two statements is true, and an equivalence (also called iff or if and only if) is true only if the two statements always have the same value – i.e. both are true or both are false.

The truth values of combinations can be shown by means of a truth table, which is a 2x2 matrix with the truth value of one statement on one side and the truth value of the other statement on the other side. If we consider p and q to be two statements, then the truth values of various combinations of these two statements would be as shown in Figure 2.

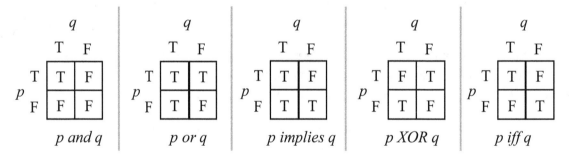

Figure 2. Truth values for some common combination of statements

In addition to the binary combinations, there is an operation on statements that is applied to a single statement, namely negation. The negation of a statement is true if the statement is false, and false if the statement in true.

The statement 'p and not p' can never be true and is always false. The statement 'p or not p' is always true and is an example of a tautology – defined as a statement that is always true.

Table 1. Some common conventions for logical operations

Operation	And	OR	Implies	IFF	XOR	Not
Convention 1	∧	∨	⇒	⇔	⊻	¬
Convention 2	&	|	→	↔	⊕	~
Convention 3	&&	||	→	↔	⊕	!

For the sake of brevity, the statements combinations are often expressed using some operator symbols. There are a few different conventions for these operators as shown in Table 1.

Proofs can be created using the logic above and valid rules of inference. The valid rules of inference allow one to derive statements that will be true starting from the axioms. Some of the valid rules of inference include:

- *Adjunction*: if p is true; and q is true; then one can infer that p ∧ q is also true.

- *Addition*: if p is true; then one can infer that p ∨ q is true.

- *Simplification*: if p ∧ q is true; then one can infer that p is also true (and q is also true).

- *Modus ponens*: if p ⇒ q is true; and p is true; then one can infer that q is true.

- *Modus tollens*: if p ⇒ q is true; and q is false; then one can infer that p is false.

- *Transitive Inference*: if p ⇒ q is true; and q ⇒ r is true; then one can infer that q ⇒ r.

- *Disjunction*: If p ∨ q is true; and q is false; then one can infer that p is true.

Proofs are constructed by using these and other valid rules of inference to derive new statements from axioms – statements that are known to be true.

A set of statements are considered consistent if they can all be true at the same time. If we consider statements that are not formed by combining other statements and call them as predicates, it means that the predicates can be assigned value of either true or false in a manner so that all the statements in the set become true.

If there are N predicates that are used in creation of a set of statements, then they may make up to 2^N possible values of true or false. If any one of these combinations result in a set of statements becoming true, that set of statements is consistent. If none of these 2^N combinations result in all the statements in the set becoming true, the set of statements is considered inconsistent. They can never all be true together.

As a simple example, the set containing two statements p and 'not p' can never be consistent.

For this course, we will simply use intuitive arguments using the valid inference approaches allowed by the formal predicate logic, instead of forcing predicate logic proofs. The reason being that formal proofs are often lengthy. Here is an illustrative example.

IT departments are notorious for giving responses that are technically correct but extremely confusing for the layperson. A new employee gave his Mac laptop, Windows Server and Android phone to the IT department and asked which one he should expect to get first. The IT person replied with this message – "If the MacBook is not the first one, then the Android one would be the first one". Confused by this response, the employee asked the IT person to clarify and got this response – "If the Windows is not the first one, then the MacBook will be the first one". Given that the IT department always speaks the truth, can you help the employee figure out which device will be returned first.

To determine the answer, we will use the following prepositions:

M → MacBook will be returned first

A → Android will be returned first

W → Windows will be returned first

The IT department response can be summarized as:

$$\sim M \Rightarrow A \qquad (1)$$
$$\sim W \Rightarrow M \qquad (2)$$

We can add to these two the general awareness of the world:

$A \vee M \vee W$	(3) One of the three must happen
$A \Rightarrow \sim M$	(4) If Android is first, MacBook cannot be first
$A \Rightarrow \sim W$	(5) If Android is first, Windows cannot be first
$W \Rightarrow \sim A$	(6) If Windows is first, Android cannot be first
$W \Rightarrow \sim M$	(7) If Windows is first, MacBook cannot be first
$M \Rightarrow \sim A$	(8) If MacBook is first, Android cannot be first
$M \Rightarrow \sim W$	(9) If MacBook is first, Windows cannot be first

Now one can derive the logic from these propositions as follows:

$M \vee A$	(10) replace 1 with its equivalent
$W \vee M$	(11) replace 2 with its equivalent

$(M \vee A) \wedge (W \vee M)$	(12) adjunction on 10 and 11
$\sim A \vee \sim M$	(13) replacing 4 with its equivalent
$\sim (A \wedge M)$	(14) alternative version of 13
$\sim W \vee \sim M$	(15) replacing 7 with its equivalent
$\sim (M \wedge W)$	(16) alternative version of 15
$\sim A \vee \sim W$	(17) replacing 5 with its equivalent
$\sim (M \wedge W)$	(18) alternative version of 15
$M \vee (M \wedge W) \vee (A \wedge M) \vee (A \wedge W)$	(19) – expanding and distributing 12
M	(20) combine 19 with 14, 16 and 18

This means that MacBook will be returned first.

While the proof is rigorous, the derivation is tedious. In this book we will use informal argument instead of proving everything using propositional logic. Our informal proofs can be converted into propositional logic if needed.

In this case, the informal argument will be the following: – The IT department first said it is either MacBook or Android. Then the second time it said, it is either MacBook or Windows. Since only one of the three can be returned first, the two statements can only be true if MacBook is the first one to be returned.

The informal arguments in this book does not necessarily mean a lack of rigor. If needed, GenAI tools can be used to convert informal arguments into a more rigorous set of propositional logic proofs.

Proof by Contradiction

Proof by contradiction is a specific method for proving a statement. To prove a statement p, one shows that assuming the 'not p' results in an inconsistent set of statements.

A common use-case of the proof of contradiction is to show that a number is irrational. A rational number is one that can be expressed as the ratio of two integers. When one needs to show that a number (e.g. $\sqrt{3}$) is irrational, one starts with the negation of that, namely that the number is rational. It implies that the number can be expressed as a ratio of a/b where we can further state that a and b are the smallest such integers. A contradiction can be obtained if we can show that the a and b are not the smallest such integers.

This is done by performing an operation that will result in the number transforming into another rational number. To show that square-roots of a number is irrational, squaring both of the sides can be the operation. In this case, the logical derivations are as follows:

$$\sqrt{3} = a/b$$

$$3 = a^2/b^2$$

$$3\,b^2 = a^2$$

Now, this means that a^2 is a multiple of 3. This in turn implies that a is a multiple of 3. Since a^2 is square number and b^2 is a factor of a^2, there must be a 3 within the factors of b^2 as well, and if b^2 is a multiple of 3 then b is a multiple of 3 as well. This means that both a and b are multiples of 3, and then a and b are not the smallest number such that $\sqrt{3}$ = a/b. The same relationship will hold true for a/3 and b/3 as well, which are smaller than a and b respectively.

This sentence contradicts with the original assumption that a and b are smallest integers. Because of the contradiction, the original assumption that $\sqrt{3}$ is irrational must be false.

The same logic can be used to show that $\sqrt{k}$ is irrational when k is any number that is not a square of an integer.

To be completely formal, the proof must be written as propositions with truth values and the results derived using the formal inference rules discussed earlier. However, for the purpose of this course, we will stick with the informal logical argument as given above. If needed, we can ask a GenAI model to convert the informal logic into a formal proof using propositions.

Some other common statements that can be proven by contradiction include:

- There are an infinite number of prime numbers.

- For any rational number a/b, there is another rational number which is smaller than a/b.

- In a party, more than 3 people were invited. Some were friends and some were strangers. At least two people in the party had the same number of friends.

- The sum of two odd numbers is an even number.

- Every positive integer greater than 2 must have a prime factor.

Exercise 1.   Use the technique of proof by contradiction to show each of the statements above. Use a GenAI tool to derive the proof if that proves helpful.

Sequences, Sums and Limits

When trying to understand the performance of various algorithms, we will often end up addressing problems of the following nature:

An algorithm operates in multiple loops. In the first loop, it performs n operations, in the second loop, it performs n-1 operations, in the third loop it performs n-2 operations and so on, stopping when there are no operations to perform. How many operations in total does the algorithm perform?

In other words, we need to determine the value of n + (n-1) + (n-2) + ... 1. Instead of simply being the sum of something that is decreasing the value at each step could be some other function, e.g. halving n or dividing n by a fixed number k etc.

If we write out the sequence in both the forward and reverse order:

$$S = 1 + 2 + 3 \ldots + (n\text{-}1) + n$$

$$S = n + (n\text{-}1) + (n\text{-}3) + \ldots 1$$

$$2S = (n{+}1) + (n{+}1) + \ldots (n{+}1)$$

$$2S = n\,(n{+}1)$$

$$S = n(n{+}1)/2$$

Another common sequence that is found is:

$$1 + r + r^2 + r^3 + \ldots + r^n$$

In this case, the sum consists of terms that are being multiplied in a ratio r. This sum can be calculated as follows:

$$S = 1 + r + r^2 + r^3 + \ldots + r^n$$

$$rS = \quad r + r^2 + r^3 + \ldots + r^n + r^{n+1}$$

Taking the difference between these two lines, we get:

$$(1\text{-}r)S = 1\text{-} r^{n+1}$$

Or S = $(1\text{-} r^{n+1})/(1\text{-}r)$

Sum of sequences can also be written using the Σ notation, which stands for summation. The two sequences discussed in this section can be written as:

$$\sum_{i=0}^{i=n} i = \frac{n(n + 1)}{2}$$

and

$$\sum_{i=0}^{i=n} r^i = \frac{(1 - r^{n+1})}{(1 - r)}$$

Proof by Induction

Proof by induction is a method that is useful for proving statements about sequences. Suppose the sequence is of length n. The approach is to show that the statement holds when n is a small number, such as 1, 2, or 3. This step is called the base case. In the next step, called the induction step, one assumes that the statement is valid when the sequence length is less than or equal to n, and shows that the statement holds true when k is n+1.

In the previous section, we showed that the following relation is valid:

$$\sum_{i=0}^{i=n} i = \frac{n(n+1)}{2}$$

We can prove this statement using induction in the following manner:

Base Step:

- For n = 1, the sum is 1 and the right hand side is 1.2/2 = 1, so the statement is true.

- For n = 2, 1 + 2 = 3 and right hand side is 2. 3/2 = 3, so the statement is true.

Induction Step:

Suppose the statement holds for all sequences up to n, which implies that:

$$1 + 2 + \ldots + n = n(n+1)/2$$

For n + 1:

$$1+2 + \ldots + (n+1)$$
$$= (1+2 + \ldots + n) + (n+1)$$
$$= n(n+1)/2 + (n+1)$$
$$= [(n+1)n + 2 (n+1)]/2$$
$$= (n+1)(n+2)/2$$

Since both the base step and the induction step are valid, the statement is valid for all values of n.

Using proof by induction, many relationships can be proven such as:

- $\sum_{i=1}^{i=n} i^2 = \frac{n(n+1)(2n+1)}{6}$

- $11^n - 6$ is divisible by 5 whenever n is a positive integer

16

- $2^n > 2n$ for all $n > 2$

- $n^3 - n$ is a multiple of 6 for all positive integers n greater or equal to 2

- $n^3 + 2n$ is a multiple of 3 for all positive integers n greater than 0

- $\sum_{i=1}^{i=n} i^2 = \frac{n(n+1)(2n+1)}{6}$

- $\sum_{i=1}^{i=n} i^3 = \frac{n^2(n+1)^2}{4}$

- $\sum_{i=1}^{i=n} \frac{1}{i(i+1)} = \frac{n}{n+1}$ for all positive integers n greater or equal to 2

> **Exercise 2.** Use induction to show that each of the statements above is true. Use a GenAI tool if you find that helpful in the proof.

Chapter Summary/Key Takeaways

Properties of computer algorithms and data structures can be proven formally using predicate logic and inference rules. In this book, however, we will focus on the informal proofs that represent the same logic in an informal manner.

Proof by contradiction and proof by induction are two common techniques that can be used to prove statements about performance of algorithms. Usually, this requires proving properties about sequences that measure some attributes of the algorithms.

In the next chapter, we will explore how performance of algorithms is measured using approximation notations.

References

[1] Lehman, E., Leighton, F.T. and Meyer, A.R., *Mathematics for computer science*. Massachusetts Institute of Technology, 2015

[2] Reeves S., Logic for Computer Science. 2003.

Chapter 3.   Analysis of Computer Algorithms

When solving any problem using computer software, it is important that the software be written to run efficiently. The use and study of almost any aspect of computer software requires an understanding of the principles that make software programs work well.

A computer software consists of a set of instructions that are written down in some type of programming language. These instructions follow a well-defined logic which is the algorithm implemented in the software. The software usually takes an input and produces an output. The software needs a physical hardware to run. The time it takes for the software to convert the input to output depends on several factors, including the size of the input, the characteristics (speed, memory, disk space) of the available hardware, as well as the complexities of processing the input and the logic of the software. Since all of these vary significantly, obtaining an accurate estimate of the running time of a software is a difficult task.

For the performance analysis, there will be a liberal use of *engineering approximations*. Engineering approximations are a common approach to simplify the complexity that comes up in the real world. The idea behind the engineering approximation is to simplify the problem that is to be solved but do it in a manner so that the problem can still be solved reasonably well. Equivalently, one can quote a line from Albert Einstein – ""Make everything as simple as possible but no simpler."

Suppose a program is given an input of size n and it completes the processing in time t. Since the program is a definite concrete set of steps, it should always complete the processing in the same amount of time if it is run on the same computer hardware which is fully devoted to the task of running that program only. The processing time is uniquely determined by the input size n and we can say that the time of program execution is a function of n, which is shown in short form as $f(n)$. Instead of using the variable f, one can use other letters to denote a function such as $g(n)$ or $t(n)$.

In a real-world computer, many programs share the hardware and running times of same program can vary depending on what other programs are running. Nevertheless, understanding the function of running time as it depends on input size is useful in comparing software systems.

Note that the input size relevant to the software or the algorithm would depend on the specifics of the algorithm. If a program translates a phrase from English to Spanish, then the relevant input size is the length of the phrase. If a program is taking a social security number and searching for that number from records maintained in a database, the relevant input size is the number of records stored in the database.

While it is not possible to always get an estimate of the actual time to run a program, one can get a rough estimate of the impact on the time required to run the program when the size of input is varied. For example, one can estimate that is the size of the input is doubled, a program takes four times as long to run as the original running time.

Even with this simplification of considering the variation in running time as a function of input size, considerable complexity still exists with estimating the running time. Software programs are complex entities with conditional branches, loops that continue until some conditions are satisfied, and complex sequences of subroutine calls. Determining the run-time function is a hard challenge and, in many cases, virtually impossible. The next engineering approximation is to analyze the function only when the input size is *large*. In a mathematical sense large would mean the value of the function $f(n)$ as n approaches infinity.

The next engineering approximation is to not examine the exact function for large value of n but examine bounding functions. A bounding function is a simpler function which can be shown to be either larger or smaller than the actual function. This leads to the O and Ω notations for program analysis.

Bounding Functions: O and Ω

The actual function which characterizes the running time of an algorithm can be a very complex one. Some examples of what that function may look like are shown in Figure 3.

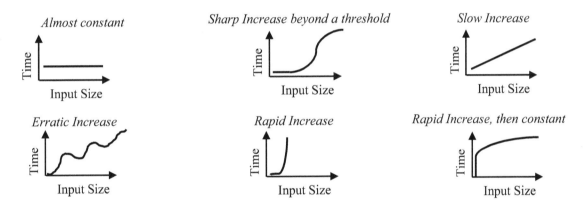

Figure 3. Some examples of increase in running time

The running time in some cases may not be dependent on the size of the input. If we consider a program which is used to select the first record from a collection of records, the running time of that program would be almost constant, regardless of how large the collection of records was. This will result in an almost constant function.

A program that returns fixed number of records (say K records) from a collection may work very fast when the number of records is small enough to be held entirely in memory but increase sharply if the number of records in the collection requires storing some of the records on the disk storage of the computer. This will result in a function which has a sharp increase beyond some threshold.

Another program may increase linearly with the number of records, e.g. a program that is trying to find the maximum of a field in the collection and needs to look at each record at least once. This will show a gradual increase in the running time as a function of the input size.

In other cases, the logic of the program may cause some erratic changes in the running time if it switches its logic in a dynamic varied pattern. Other programs may increase very sharply as the number of collection records increase, while others may increase rapidly with the collection size for some threshold and then stabilize to a constant value.

Instead of trying to estimate the exact running time of an algorithm, program analysis tries to establish bounds on the actual functions. The actual bound could be either an upper bound or a lower bound. A function $f(n)$ is bounded on the upper side by another function $g(n)$ if $g(n)$ is always greater than $f(n)$ for all values of n. Similarly, a function $f(n)$ is bounded on the lower side by another function $h(n)$ if $h(n)$ is always smaller than $f(n)$ for all values of n. An example of the bounding functions on the upper side and lower side is shown in Figure 4.

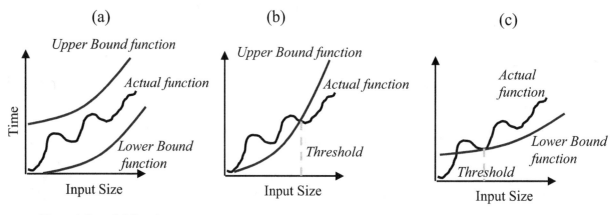

Figure 4. Bounded Functions

The first among the three figures shown in Figure 4, i.e. (a) shows a complex function with a function that is bounding it from above and a function which is bounding it from below. The advantage of having a bounding function is that we can have a simpler function that acts as the upper bound or as the lower bound and we do not need to worry about the complexities of the actual function.

The actual function may be a complex expression in terms of the input size n, e.g. f(n) may have the form of $f(n) = 32n^{78} - 35n^{56} + 37n^{36} - x^2 + 278$. In contrast the upper bound function may be something simpler, e.g. $f(n) = n^{100}$. A simpler expression is easier to both estimate and compare with other functions.

Some of the typical functions in a simplified form that are commonly used are shown in the table below:

Function	Common Name	Notes
$y = c$	Constant	c is a constant value
$y = c.n$	Linear	y is proportional to n
$y = c.n^2$	Quadratic	Is a special case of the polynomial
$y = c.\log(n)$	Logarithm	The log can be taken for any base
$y = c.n^k$	Polynomial	The exponent k is a constant
$y = c.2^x$	Exponential	One of the fastest growing functions

You may notice that none of the functions have any coefficients or constants. This is another type of simplification which can be made. We are not typically interested in finding a function which is bounding (either from above or below) all the time, but only a function which bounds the real function when the input n is large. This is a function that is an upper bound for large values, even if the relationship may not hold for smaller values of the input n. An example of such a function is shown in Figure 4 (b). Similarly, a function that acts like the lower bound for large values, but not for the small values, like the example shown in Figure 4 (c).

The asymptotic bounds are expressed using the O and Ω notations. When a function $f(n)$ is bounded asymptotically (i.e. for large values of the input) from above by another function $g(n)$ we say that $f(n)$ is O($g(n)$). If the function $f(n)$ is bounded from below by another function $g(n)$, we say that $f(n)$ is Ω ($g(n)$).

The more formal and precise definitions are as follows:

- $f(n) = O(g(n))$ means that there exists some number n_0 and some constant c such that whenever $n > n_0$, $f(n) < c.g(n)$

- $f(n) = \Omega$ ($h(n)$) means that there exists some number n_0 and some constant c such that whenever $n > n_0$, $f(n) > c.h(n)$

These definitions also make our tasks easier in that we can only focus on a handful of functions to discuss the asymptotic complexity of the functions. A generic function can be a combination of many functions, but for the purpose of managing bounds, only the larger of those components need to be considered.

Here are some examples of O and Ω functions:

- $3n^4 + 2n^3 + 5n + 70$ is $O(n^4)$. This is because as *n* becomes large, the highest power function dominates, and the coefficient can be dropped. One can choose the value of n_0 to be 1000, and the constant *c* to be 4 as per the formal definition.

- $3n^4 + 2n^3 + 5n + 70$ is $\Omega(n^4)$. This is because as *n* becomes large, the highest power function dominates, and the coefficient can be dropped. One can choose the value of n_0 to be 1000, and the constant *c* to be 2 as per the formal definition.

When estimating the upper and lower bounding functions, it is best to use the power that gives the tightest bound. A function that is $O(n^4)$ is also $O(n^5)$ and $O(n^6)$, but one should use the lowest possible power. Similarly, a function that is $\Omega(n^4)$ is also $\Omega(n^3)$ and $\Omega(n^2)$ but the highest power would be used.

If $f(n) = O(g(n))$ and $f(n) = \Omega(g(n))$ then we say that $f(n) = \Theta(g(n))$. Θ becomes the average running time for very large values of input since $g(n)$ becomes an approximation of the actual function in the asymptotic case.

From the perspective of analyzing the behavior of a program, which may go through different portions of program logic, the O function marking the performance of the program gives its worst-case performance – what it would perform asymptotically for very large input in the worst case. Similarly, the Ω function characterizing the program indicates the best-case performance of the algorithm in the asymptotic case – i.e. when the size of the input is very large. In between these two extremes, Θ function defines the average running time of the algorithm in the asymptotic case.

Performance of Some Functions

In this section, we will look at the run-time performance of some simple programs. As the first example, we can consider the code that computes the smallest number among a set of numbers. The program can be written with several implicit assumptions. One of the assumptions here would be whether the input contains numbers that are already sorted in an increasing order, sorted in a decreasing order, or unsorted. Another assumption would be how much time it takes to access a number in the set at a given position.

In order to keep the discussion at a broad level, we will be writing the programs in a very generic language instead of a specific language. We will leave it as an exercise for the reader to convert these simple programs into concrete executable code in some language. (Hint: you can use any of the GenAI services on the Internet to do this translation).

To show that the program is written in a generic language, we will be showing each program in a bounded box with four headings – the name of the program, the assumptions made for the program, the problem solved by the program, and the logic of the program.

Using these conventions, our first program is.

Name: find1
Assumptions
   (i) Input is a set of sorted numbers from smallest to largest
   (ii) It takes a constant amount of time to read any number from the set
Problem:
   Find the smallest number in the set
Logic:
   Return the first number in the set

This program will have a constant running time. This is because the first number in the set is the smallest one, and it takes a constant amount of time to return the first number. With these set of assumptions, even if the set were sorted from largest to smallest, we would have a constant running time since we would simply lookup the last item in the set, and that lookup can be done in a constant time.

We can change the assumptions, and the program would have a different running time.

Name: find2
Assumptions
   (i) Input is a set of sorted numbers from largest to smallest
   (ii) The amount of time taken to read a number is proportional to its position in the set
Problem:
   Find the smallest number in the set
Logic:
   Return the last number in the set

In this case, the amount of time it takes to read the last number in the set is $O(n)$ if the size of the input set is n. This means that the running time of this algorithm would be O(n). Note that this result is dependent on the assumption that the time taken to read a number is proportional to its position in the set. If we assumed that the time taken to read a number is constant, then the running time of the find2 program would be O(constant).

Exercise 3.   What would be the running time of the program find2 if its problem was to find the largest number in the set, and the logic was to return the first number in the set?

Most programming languages support the notion of a loop in which a variable repeats through multiple entries in a list of numbers. The loop may terminate when a condition is met, an example of the condition being that all the entries in the list have been considred. In general, each nesting of the loop adds one exponent to the running time of the program. The semi-structured logic of the programs below, which is written in semi-natural language can illustrate some of these:

Name: print_squares
Assumptions
    (i) Input is a set of numbers in a list
    (ii) The amount of time taken to read a number is constant
    (iii) The amount of time taken to multiply two numbers or print a number is constant
Problem:
    Print squares of all numbers in a list:
Logic:
    for each entry x in the list
        y = square of x
        print y

The above program goes through all the entries in the list once and will be $O(n)$ since it is going through each of the n items once.

On the other hand, if the program were going through each of the items and printing the square of each item using two loops, it would have $O(n^2)$ runtime since it is comparing each item against another item.

Name: multiply_squares
Assumptions
    (i) Input is a set of numbers in a list
    (ii) The amount of time taken to read a number is constant
    (iii) The amount of time taken to multiply two numbers or print a number is constant
Problem:
    Multiply all the numbers in a list and square the result
Logic:
    let answer be 1
    for each entry x in the list:
        for each entry y in the list:
            update answer to be answer multiplied by x multiplied by y
    print answer

The logic used to implement a program can be done in different manners. As long as the goal is to get the multiplication of all squares, the logic shown in multiply_squares is not unique. One can use a different logic to write a variation of the program which produces the exact same result. Different logical ways to implement the program would result in a different run time for the program.

Shown below is a program that implements an equivalent of multiply_squares to run in O(n) time:

Name: multiply_squares_2
Assumptions
   (i) Input is a set of numbers in a list
   (ii) The amount of time taken to read a number is constant
   (iii) The amount of time taken to multiply two numbers or print a number is constant
Problem:
   Multiply all the numbers in a list and square the result
Program:
   let answer be 1
   for each entry x in the list:
       update answer to be answer multiplied by x multiplied by x
   print answer

In general, the number of nested loops provides a good estimate of the running time of the program. If there are k nested loops iterating over the elements of a set, the program would have a running time of $O(n^k)$. It is for that reason that multiply_squares is $O(n^2)$ while multiply_squares2 is $O(n)$.

Because of the tremendous flexibility in loops that all programming languages provide, one can create tricky examples in which a program may appear to have multiple nested loops, but its would have a different run-time complexity.

Name: triple_membership
Assumptions
   (i) Input is a set of numbers in a list
   (ii) The amount of time taken to read a number is constant
   (iii) The amount of time taken to compare two numbers or print a number is constant
Problem:
   Given three lists listA, listB and listC, find if there is a number common in all three lists
Logic:
   for each entry a in listA:
     for each entry b in listB:
       for each entry c in listC:
         if (a equals b) and (b equals c) then print 'common entry found' and exit
   print 'no common entry exists'

An example is the problem of checking for common membership among three lists – i.e. check if a number occurs in all three of the lists. This would normally be written as an $O(n^3)$ time as shown above.

However, the same problem can also be solved using the following approach:

Logic:
    for each entry a in listA:
     for each entry b in listB:
      if (a equals b):
       for each entry c in listC:
        if (b equals c) then print 'common entry found' and exit
    print 'no common entry exists'

In this modified version of the program, the innermost loop is only executed when the entries in the lists A and B match. Since each of these two lists have n entries, the comparison can be true for only n values. This means the inner-most loop over listC will only be executed n times in the worst case and contribute $O(n^2)$ to the running complexity. The two outer loops also contribute $O(n^2)$ comparison and so the net program becomes $O(n^2)$ complexity.

In most common programming scenarios, we may not run into such tricky situations. However, it is always useful to be aware of these situations in case one runs into those types of programs.

Chapter Summary/Key Takeaways

The performance time of algorithms is analyzed by means of asymptotic performance when their input size is large. The O notation is used to characterize the worst-case asymptotic performance while the Ω notation is used to characterize the best case asymptotic performance. Ideally, the function implementation with the lowest worst time performance should be selected since that provides the fastest approach for large data.

Chapter 4.   Abstractions in Computer Science

The learning of concepts in computer science, particularly in the era of GenAI, has to be based around the idea of abstraction. An abstraction, as defined by the dictionaries, is the generalization of an idea, rather than a specific concrete form. An abstraction hides the complexity of an actual system and expresses it in a simpler manner. In computer science, the concept of abstraction is used in an analogous manner.

A computer user may use the computer for a task such as browsing the Internet, or for updating the financial records maintained in a spreadsheet, or to write a poem in a word processor. The computer user is using a software program which has been developed by a programmer.

A programmer writing a software program is in a very powerful position as far as the program is concerned. The programmer can define any entity within the world of the software program and define the behavior of the entity in any imaginable manner. The programmer creates this world to aid the user of the program. The goal of the program is to enable the user to do some tasks or activities in a better manner. The better manner could be an increase in the ease of doing the task, the time to complete the task, or decrease the cost of performing the task.

The developer of a programming language must define a similar world. The user of this programming language is the programmer mentioned in the previous program. The goal of the developer (of the programming language) is to make the task of programing easier. To attain this goal, the developer of the programming language will create a compiler or interpreter to support the task of programming.

The developer of the programming language is, in turn, the user of the developer of the operating system, who is the user of the architect of the computer hardware, who is turn is a user of the devices, processors and chips in the computer.

The net result is that there is a chain of developers and users of those developers to enable the task that a computer may be used for. Each developer offers a system to be used by its user, who in turn would use the provided system to create another system to be used by the next user in the chain. Such a chain in shown in Figure 5.

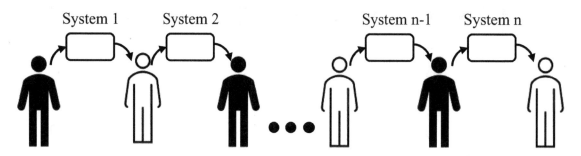

Figure 5. The chain of systems used to enable a computer-based task

Each developer can define the system being offered to his/her user. Developers want the users to use the system they are offering, and this can only be attained if the system makes the life of the user easy. A common approach to make the life of user easy is to define abstractions that simplify the effort in performing the task the user needs to do.

To put a more concrete sequence of the chain of users and developers shown in Figure 5, the original developer could be the creator of a hardware component like a disk. The user of this component (along with other components like processors and memory) would be the developer of the computer hardware system. The computer hardware system offers an abstraction known as the Von Neumann Architecture to its users. Almost all the commercial computer systems available at the present time, excluding quantum computers, follow a flavor of the Von Neumann Architecture. Using the Von Neumann Architecture as its input, the developer of a programming language such as C, Python or Java would offer a system (generally called compiler or interpreter of the language) which offers the abstractions supported by the programming language, such as named variables, procedures, loops etc. Using these abstractions, the developer of a relational database system may offer abstractions such as a stored table, database schema definition, stored queries etc. Using these abstractions in turn, the developer of an eCommerce site may offer abstractions such as products, loyalty cards and shopping carts. Those abstractions in turn would be used by sellers on the site to perform the business task of selling merchandise to their customers.

Defining abstractions

An abstraction in computer science needs to be defined with some level of specificity. The common approach to define an abstraction is to specify a name for the abstractions, and the type of operations that can be done on it. The type of operation that can be done on the abstractions also need to be defined so that they are unambiguous and can be implemented in a language.

As an example, a programming language may have an abstraction that corresponds to the mathematical concept of an integer. In mathematics, an integer is defined as an entity with a discrete value that can take values from 0, 1, 2, 3, … or the values -1, -2, -3 … etc. In computer science, an entity that can take distinct values of a similar nature can be defined as an integer. The limitations of the computer may prevent a true representation of this concept, so a computer may define an

28

abstraction called an integer which can take discrete values no more than 2147483647 and no less than -2147483648. This is the abstraction of an integer in a programming language like Java, and is given the name of int.

In addition to the name and characteristics such as maximum and minimum value, the abstraction is defined with operations that can be done on it. Such abstractions include operations that can be done on the integer entity. For example, increment and decrement operation on an abstract integer changes its value.

The definition of an abstraction gives it a name, defines constraints and characteristics associated with the definition, and defines the operations associated with the abstraction. These definitions need to be done with sufficient precision so that there is no confusion in their understanding or implementation. The specification can be done in natural language, or if a programming language is being used, by defining the interface in the programming language along with its constraints.

A very critical aspect to consider when defining an abstraction is its utility. A good abstraction would be useful – it would either make the task of an upstream developer easy by hiding complexity, allows the same software to run on many different platforms, or provide some other improvement that will be desirable. While abstractions can be defined in any arbitrary manner, good abstractions would provide some utility to someone. When defining any abstraction, it is also useful to include some justification for the existence of the abstraction, namely the utility or value that it would provide.

As an example, let us consider the definition of an abstraction called an *Encryptor*. The Encryptor supports an *encrypt* operation which takes a text string represented in Unicode of a length which is a multiple of 64 characters and produced an output string of the same length. The Encryptor supports an *initialization* operation in which it is provided a key of length 64 characters. The Encryptor also supports a *decrypt* operation which will perform the inverse of the decrypt operation.

This abstraction has a name (Encryptor), the constraints (the input to encrypt and decrypt must be strings with length of 64) a definition of three operations it supports (encrypt, decrypt, and initialize). Its utility would be to hide the complexity of converting the encryption – since the key can be used with a variety of algorithms which use the key to modify the input for encryption or decryption in different manner. The complexity of the algorithm for encryption is hidden from the user, simplifying its usage.

Implementing abstractions

A key requirement of an abstraction in computers is that they not only be defined, but that they should be implementable in terms of the abstractions available to the developer. The implementation would need to be done in a formal programming language, and the implementation is done to satisfy all the requirements of the definition of the abstraction. One can write description of the implementation in natural language so that the approach to implement it is precisely specified.

The implementation of any abstraction is done in terms of the abstractions available to the developer of the system. Almost all software developers are using another software or hardware system underneath to develop their software. This allows them to use and combine the abstractions available to them to create new abstractions.

The implementation process can be visualized as building a wall from individual bricks that are available, or for laying out the tiles on a floor using a set of available tiles. If you have tiles of different sizes, one can compose the individual tiles into a complex mosaic of patterns. If the mosaics are available to another user, it enables them to combine the mosaics into other more complex patterns. Software abstractions are defined in a similar manner, by composing them from underlying abstractions.

An illustration of the concept is shown in Figure 6. Suppose we have access to two types of tiles – a dark one and a light one. A software developer can use them to create combinations of 2x1 tiles and 2x2 tiles that are of various patterns. The composed tiles can be rotated and placed in various configurations, allowing a higher-level user of the composed mosaic of tiles to create new patterns such as a cross or a line. This allows creation of many patterns. The higher-level compositions make it easier to create more complex patterns.

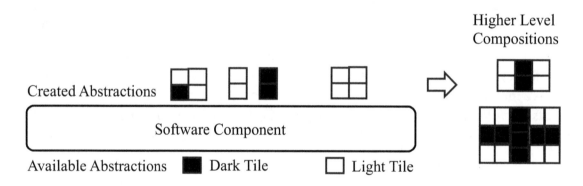

Figure 6. Illustration of composition of abstractions using tiles as examples

A key difference in the composition of software abstractions is that there is much higher degree of freedom in composing abstractions in software. The task of composition of abstractions in a physical world such as tiles or bricks is constrained by the physical laws. The laws governing software systems are much more fluid.

The implementation of an abstraction can be done in two manners. The logical implementation of the abstraction is provided by means of an algorithm – a sequence of steps that can be followed to implement the abstraction. The algorithm is independent of the exact language in which it is implemented. The other manner of implementation is a concrete implementation of the algorithm in a programming language.

For the abstraction of *Encryptor* defined earlier, we can write the implementation of initialization operation as storing the key in a local variable. On both the encrypt and decrypt operation, the contents of the key are bitwise XORed with the input argument, if the input has a length of a multiple of 64 characters. If the length does not satisfy this condition, it is an error condition. In a language that supports exceptions, an exception is raised. In a language which does not support exceptions, the implementation may specify that the operation would return -1 if the length of the argument is not met.

The above description is precise enough to be implemented in any programming language and provides a logical implementation of the abstraction. The concrete abstraction would be the implementation of the algorithm in a selected programming language.

The task of any software developer is to create new abstractions for the users who will use their software. These abstractions are implemented in terms of the lower-level abstractions that are available to the developer.

In an object-oriented programming language, each abstraction would typically be implemented as definition of a class. In such languages, the class is an abstraction that allows an easy manner to define and implement the abstraction.

In other languages, each abstraction would typically be implemented in modules, each module consisting of a set of functions that implement the abstraction.

Abstraction Definition Box

To clearly delineate the abstraction definition and abstraction implementation, we will be using a structured box to define each abstraction we encounter. The structure of the box looks like:

Abstraction Name: Array
Constraints:
 (i) any applicable constraints
Operations:
 The interface exported by the abstraction. This should specify the arguments and return values
Utility:
 A brief description of value provided by this abstraction

The name and assumptions of the abstraction should be self-explanatory. The operations define the interface of the abstraction. If a concrete language is selected, the operations would correspond to the function declaration of the abstraction.

The abstraction definition box can be equated to the function declarations in the header file of a procedural language, or defining the signature of the operations supported on a class definition in an object-oriented language. Instead of defining the exact structure, we are leaving it at a more casual level for the purposes of instruction.

Chapter Summary/Key Takeaways

This chapter covers the concept of abstractions, which are constructs developed to make the life of users easy. Each abstraction has a definition which consists of a name, a set of constraints, a set of operations, and a justification for the abstraction. The implementation of an abstraction is logically done by means of an algorithm and concretely done by a piece of software in a programming language.

While computer hardware exports the abstraction of bits and words in the computer, programming languages use them to create a higher abstraction of basic data types and a data record. Data collections are abstractions that represent a collection of data records.

In the next chapter, we will take a broad overview of some of the common data structures, and the physical analogue which has inspired their creation.

PART II: Basic Data Structures

In this part of the book, we cover the properties of some of the common data structures and how those can be used to solve some interesting problems in computer science.

The first chapter in this section provides an overview of the basic data structures and discusses the real-world analogues from which they are derived.

The next chapter covers a discussion of arrays. Arrays are the simplest type of data structures, but they are very useful to solve a variety of problems. We would discuss some of the examples where the use of arrays simplifies the logic for solving a problem.

This is followed by a chapter that covers the data structure of linked lists and its variations, such as stacks and queues.

The subsequent chapter discusses the concept of trees and some of the applications of trees in various problems.

The final chapter in this section discusses the concepts of maps and hash-tables.

Chapter 5. Common Data Structures

In this chapter, we discuss how the concept of abstractions can be customized for the specific context of data structures. This is followed by look at some of the common data structures (arrays, lists, stacks, queues, trees and maps).

For the customization of the abstractions, we consider three tiers of abstractions – the data abstraction, the data type abstraction and the data structure abstraction.

The Data Abstraction

For the developer of a programming language, the operating system or the hardware of the machine exports some basic abstractions on which new abstractions need to be developed. These basic operations include:

- A bit which can take a value of either 0 or 1

- A word which is a sequence of bits defined by the architecture of the computer

Using these two abstractions, each programming language offers the abstraction of a data type. Typical data types include items such as integers, floating point numbers, strings and characters. Specifically, the following abstractions for different types of data are described in a language like Java:

- `Byte` - stores an 8 bit number with one bit of sign

- `short` - stores an 16 bit number with one bit of sign

- `int` - stores an 16 bit number with one bit of sign

- `long` - stores an 16 bit number with one bit of sign

- `float` - stores fractional numbers using 32 bits for number representation

- `double` - stores fractional numbers using 64 bits for number representation

- `Boolean` – store true or false values

- `char` - stores a single character/letter in Unicode

Operations such as addition, subtraction, multiplication and division are defined for each data abstractions which represents the number data types. An equality comparison for all the data types

34

is also provided, and a set of logical operations such as (or, and, exclusive or, and negation) are defined for each of the Boolean data types.

The implementation of these abstractions depends on the word-size and other details of the underlying hardware. The big value of simplification offered by the programming language data type abstractions is that one can write software without worrying about the details of the underlying hardware. The same software that will work on a large mainframe will also work on a personal computer even though they have very different hardware configurations.

Data Structure Abstraction

A data structure is an abstraction that is built atop the fundamental data type abstraction offered by a programming language. The data structure abstraction allows one to compose various data types into more complex structures. These more complex structures allow one to manipulate information relevant to their needs in an easier manner.

The simplest unit of a data structure is a collection of different data types, which we will refer to as a data record. The data record is an aggregate of one or more basic data types. It allows one to handle all the units as part of a larger whole, instead of treating them differently. As an example, when developing software for a university, each student would typically have associated attributes such as a first name, a last name, middle name (or names), a student identity number and an email address. Each of these attributes are of a basic data type, the names are strings, the identity number is an integer, and the email address is a string with a specific format. In different programming languages, such an aggregate may be defined as a `record` (used in Pascal), a `struct` (used in C and C++) or a `class` (used in object-oriented languages like Java or Python).

When multiple data records are present, they can be manipulated in a variety of ways. The set can be arranged to support a variety of operations, and the efficiency of the different operations can be different depending on how they are implemented and supported. An abstraction which handles a collection of data records is a data structure. Data structures simplify the task of managing many data records.

Note that a data record can also be one of the basic data types, i.e. the data structure which is used to manipulate a set of data records can also be used for a collection of integers, or a collection of strings. The properties of the data structure remain similar regardless of what an individual data record may contain. It also follows that a data record might be another data structure, in which case the data structure is a collection of many different data structures.

The common operations that all data structures would need to support are:

- Creating and initializing a new instance of the data structure

- Adding data record to the data structure

- Checking if a data record exists in the data structure

- Removing a data record from the data structure

- Finding the number of data records in the data structure

The time it takes to perform any one of these operations would vary depending on how the records are managed and maintained within the data structure. Different types of data structures would have different run-time. As an example, consider two data structures A and B, each of which contain n data records. In data structure A, the time to add another record could be O(n) while in data structure B, the time to add another record could be O(constant). If a majority of operations are record additions, data structure B would be the preferred one to use.

Common types of data structures include arrays, lists, stacks, queues, trees and maps. They are covered in detail in the subsequent chapters of this book.

An analogy can be drawn between data structures and collections of books. A collection of books contains many different books. Different people may choose different ways to store their books. An individual who is not very organized may just put all the books in a pile on a desk. Adding a new book to the collection would be easy, just toss the book on to the pile of books on the desk and it will take constant amount of time. Finding if a book is in the collection requires going through all the books in the pile and take O(n) time if there are n books in the pile.

On the other hand, these books can be arranged and indexed in a variety of ways. An individual may decide to sort the books into different piles depending on the language in which the book is written or put them on a bookshelf sorted by the last name of the author, or put them on a bookshelf with each shelf containing books on a different subject. The amount of time to add a book in these cases would be longer, but finding books would be much faster than arranging them in a haphazard pile. Different data structures correspond to different types of arrangements of books that are possible.

Arrays

An array maintains a collection of records in a manner inspired by the setup of mailboxes that can be found in housing complexes that contain multiple apartments. A housing complex consisting of N apartments would generally number the apartments from 1 to N. The housing complex mailboxes may be arranged either in the pattern of street mailboxes put together in a row, or in the pattern of mailbox units that are arranged in a 2-dimensional grid. Both configurations are shown in Figure 7.

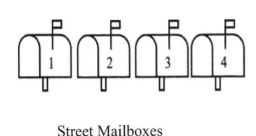

Street Mailboxes

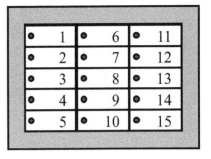

Apartment Complex Mailboxes

Figure 7 Two common configuration of mailboxes in an apartment complex

When a parcel is to be delivered to the apartment, it can be placed in the appropriately numbered mailbox. When the parcel is to be retrieved, one can open the corresponding mailbox and retrieve it. The approach works for both arrangements of the mailboxes.

Arrays are modeled after the same physical arrangement where the parcel to be put into the mailbox is a data record, and the array models the entire collection of the mailboxes. The array can be either a single dimension, or it can be modeled as mailboxes distributed along two or more dimensions. In a software driven world, any number of dimensions can be implemented easily, unlike the physical world which is limited to three dimensions.

In the physical world, an array of mailboxes would have a fixed capacity. There are only a finite number of elements in a row of mailboxes. In the software world, arrays can be defined to have a fixed capacity. Following the adage that software world need not follow physical world laws, software-based arrays can be defined to have unlimited capacity as well.

Arrays are perhaps the simplest data structure that can be envisioned, yet they are incredibly useful. They can serve as the building block for creating many complex abstractions and solving interesting problems.

Lists

A list is modeled after the real-world artifact of shopping lists, mailing lists, or any other type of lists that people maintain including Santa Claus's nice list and naughty list. The lists maintained in the real-world have no limit of the capacity and have no order among the elements of the list. An example of a shopping list is shown in Figure 8. Of the three items shown in the figure, one item has been checked off indicating that it has been purchased, and the others are still to be purchased.

✓	Apples
	Bananas
	Oranges

Figure 8. An example of a shopping list

A software list is an abstraction which maintains data records in an unordered manner and allows any number of data records to be inserted into the list. Data records are not maintained in any order. For the specific case shown in Figure 8, a data record would contain two data types, an item to be purchased which would be a string, and an indicator of its status which would be a Boolean.

A list is an important data structure and provides the foundational building block that helps in building other complex data structures. In other words, the list abstraction is useful as a building block for many other different types of abstractions.

Queues

A queue is familiar from many of real-world experience when several people require some type of service to be done. Whether people are waiting to purchase their items at a grocery store, or waiting to board a bus, or waiting to renew their driving licenses at the department of motor vehicles, the creation of a queue is a common occurrence. A queue of people waiting to board a bus is shown in Figure 9.

The real-world queue has some unique properties. It has a person at the head of the queue, and a person at the end of the queue. The order of each person in the queue is determined by when they join. Every person joins at the end of the queue. As the person at the front of the queue leaves the queue, the person who joined the queue after that comes to the head. The order of departure of people from the queue is in the first in first out (FIFO) order.

The computer representation of a queue follows the similar structure as that of the real world. Data records are put into the queue in a first in first out order. The queue maintains the concept of a head and a tail. People are only allowed to join at the tail of the queue. When a record must be taken out, the entry at the head of the queue is taken out.

Figure 9. A Queue of people waiting to board a bus

As in real-life, queue data structure is very useful to maintain the information when some entities need to be provided a service, but the service provider is busy. Those entities that must wait for the service are put into a queue data structure. Such entities can be processes trying to access a resource such as a printer. Since printing content is slow compared to other operations within a computer, such processes are put into a queue so that they can be serviced when the printer becomes available.

Stacks

We encounter many instances of a stack in real life. Coins are often stacked together in piles of equal height so that they are easy to count. Books on our desk may be stacked on top of each other. During breakfast, one may order a stack of pancakes. Other examples of stacks include a stack of washed plates or a stack of glasses that are put together for use.

Figure 10. Some stacks in real-life – a stack of coins, a stack of books and a stack of pancakes.

The stack has some properties that are in a complete contrast when compared to a queue. Items are placed on top of the queue and removed from the top of the queue. As a result, the item that is placed last in the queue is the first one to be taken out. The order for entering and exiting the stack is last in first out or the LIFO order.

Computer implementations of stacks follow the same construct as real-life construct with items getting popped from the top of the stack and getting pushed on top of the stack in the LIFO order.

Trees

Trees in computer software development are modeled after real-life trees, but with some distinct differences. A tree in real-life has a root, a trunk and then some branches. The branches keep on dividing into sub-branches until they end with leaves at the tip of the sub-branches.

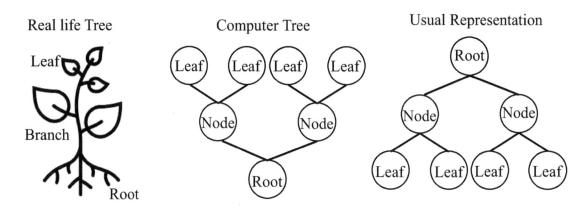

Figure 11. A real-life tree with roots, branches and leaves. The middle diagram shows corresponding concepts of root, leaves and nodes at branches as analogues to real-life tree. The right-most diagram shows how trees are normally represented in computer science books.

In a real-life tree, the root is at the bottom of the tree, with the leaves being at the top. In computer science, the data records are placed at various locations in a tree called nodes. A node that does not branch any further is called a leaf. The node which is the bottom-most in the real-life analogue would be called the root. This follows the analogy of a real-world tree quite closely.

By convention, in computer science the root node is shown at the top and the leaves shown in the bottom as demonstrated in the right-most diagram of the computer. There is no logical difference in the two representations and this book will follow the traditional convention and show all trees with the root at the top.

Maps

A map in real-life is used to show the layout of a place, e.g. at all national parks a map of the park is shown with symbols showing various facilities. At the side of the map is an index which provides an explanation for what the symbols on the map mean. Within a library system before automation using computers, a set of index cards were maintained that showed where books on a particular subject or written by a particular author may be found. The basic purpose of the map or index card is to ease the process of finding information. Two examples of such maps in real-life are shown in Figure 12.

Figure 12. Some examples of map structures in real life

The map data structure provides the same function in software. It consists of a set of data records that can be looked up using a key. This allows one to find data records using the index information. In many ways, the map is like an array but whereas an array only has an integer as a key to lookup data records, a map can have an arbitrary type of key (e.g. a string or even a picture) to lookup a record by its key.

The flexibility to use other data types as an index provides a significant degree of convenience to the end software developer by eliminating the need to maintain a mapping from the intuitive key value to an integer index which can then be used to lookup information in an array.

Common Operations

On all data structures, a few common operations are always supported. Sometimes, these operations may need additional arguments. These operations are summarized in the table below.

Operation	Explanation	Notes
create	Create a new instance of data structure	May often need configuration parameters. This usually results in a data structure without any records.
add	Add a data record to the data structure	Some data structures need additional arguments specifying where to add.
search /find	Search if a data record is present in the data structure	Requires that data records be comparable to do the search, i.e. given two data records, we know how to tell if they are identical or different.
remove	Remove a data record from the structure	Some data structures have special names for remove operation.

destroy	Destroy the data structure instance	In some languages, the destroy command may not be needed. Languages that implement automatic garbage collection of unused memory and objects may not always have a destroy operation.
size	Find the number of records in data structure.	It is usually a O(constant) operation. Any implementation can keep track of the number of records that are added or removed to keep track of current records in the data structure.
isempty	Does the data structure contain any records?	It is a convenience routine equivalent to getting the size and comparing that it is 0.

In addition to the above, data structures may have specific operations. In some cases, the operations may be called differently, e.g. in a stack, the add and remove operations are called push and pop.

Chapter Summary/Key Takeaways

In this chapter, we have looked at the inspiration behind the data structures that we will be covering in this class. The data structures that we provided an analog in real-life included arrays, lists, stacks, queues, trees and maps.

In the next few chapters, we will go into each of these data structures in more depth, with a close look at the types of abstractions that we can use the data structures to solve.

Chapter 6.   The Array Data Structure

The array data structure is the first data structure that we will examine in depth. We would look at its definition and its implementation, along with some other abstractions that we can define using arrays. Despite their simplicity, arrays are incredibly powerful and can act as a basis to develop many interesting computer software systems.

Definition

An array is an ordered collection of data records. In this collection there are a sequence of numeric indexes usually indexed 0, 1, 2 … and each index contains a data record of the same type. A data record can be stored in the array by providing the index at which it is stored. A data record stored at an index can be retrieved by specifying the index which is being looked at.

The constraints of the array generally include the following:

• All data records stored in the array are of the same type

• The indexes are contiguous series of positive integers starting from 0 onward.

• The array has a fixed capacity

Some variations can be defined on the basic definition above which we will consider later in the chapter.

The utility of the array is that it provides a way to easily store and retrieve data records in a collection, thereby enabling many different abstractions to be defined using it.

The operations supported by an array are:

• Create a new instance of an array. Usually this requires specifying the capacity of the array.

• Store a record at an index

• Retrieve a record stored at an index

• Delete the record stored at an index

The element at the ith location in an array A is usually referred to as A[i]. In most languages, assignment operations can be used to assign a data record to A[i] and A[i] can be used within operations allowed by the language on variables of the appropriate type.

Since this book will focus a lot on defining new abstractions using array, we will restate the same definition in a summary format as shown in the box below:

Data Structure Name: Array
Constraints:
   (i) Collection has a fixed capacity
   (ii) Accessing any index beyond the capacity results in an error condition
Operations:
   Create instance specifying capacity, store a record at index, retrieve record at index, delete record at index
Utility:
   Easy way to handle a collection of records via index

Implementation

The implementation of arrays is usually provided by the programming language itself or via special libraries that implement the array class. In most modern languages, support for arrays for basic types is provided as a standard feature. The declaration depends on the syntax of the language. In Java for example one can declare arrays of basic types such as integers as shown below:

```
// define a new empty array
int[] example_1 = new int[10];

// define a new complete array
int[] example_2 = { 1, 2, 3, 4, 5, 6 };

// Assign elements within an array
for (int i = 0; i < 10; i++) {
example_1[i] = 2 * i;
}
```

The first line in the code block defines an array of empty integer with a capacity of 10. One can also define an array of integers (or any basic type in Java) by explicitly naming the values in the array. The assignment is done in the manner of assigning any other variable using the index along with the name of the array.

To support the implementation of the array, the programming language developer would typically use a continuous block of memory. In the case of defining an array of 10 integers, since each integer in Java takes up 4 bytes (32 bits), the system will allocate a memory size of 4*10 or 40 bytes. Suppose the block is allocated at memory location m. The first integer (index 0) is stored at the beginning of the allocated block in bytes from m to m+3, the second integer (index 10 in the array at bytes m+4 to byte m+7 and so on with the i+1th integer (index i) stored at byte m+4i to m+4i+3.

Many programming languages support libraries which provide an implementation of arrays and other data structures. As an example, in Java, the collections package provides an implementation of various data structures.

Multi-Dimensional Arrays

The abstraction for arrays as defined earlier only considered arrays to have a single index. The index ranged from 0 and was allowed to take values up to the capacity of the array. In effect, it defined an array with only one dimension of the index.

For convenience of usage, it would be good to have an array be allowed to have an index which is specified in multiple dimensions. For example, let us consider an application which needs to deal with planning the motion of a robot used for cleaning a room. The robot can move on the floor of the room. It would be easier to deal with the position of the robot if we were to specify it using two coordinates, one along the x axis and one along the y axis as shown in Figure 13.

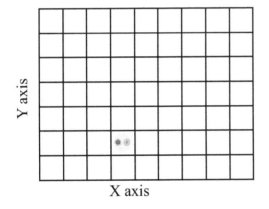

54	55	56	57	58	59	60	61	62
45	46	47	48	49	50	51	52	53
36	37	38	39	40	41	42	43	44
27	28	29	30	31	32	33	34	35
18	19	20	21	22	23	24	25	26
9	10	11	12	13	14	15	16	17
0	1	2	3	4	5	6	7	8

Figure 13. Modeling the location of a robot in a room

The left side of the Figure shows a room which is 9 units long and 7 units wide. The length is measured along the X-axis and the width along the Y-axis. A robot moves around the room. The position of the robot can be modeled as a single dimensional array with numbering as shown on right side of the figure. However, the index that results is somewhat unintuitive. It would be easier to model the room with two numbers along the X and the Y axis respectively, and position (4, 2) is easier to understand in this context than position 12.

It would make life of the programmer easier if arrays can be defined to have two dimensions so that we can easily reference the two dimensions above. In other type of problems, we may need

45

three dimensions, e.g. if we were modeling the layout of a building which is in three dimensions or modeling the movement of planets and stars for astronomic calculations. One can even have situations where we need much larger dimensions. In artificial intelligence applications, it is convention to represent text strings as points in a space that takes a thousand dimensions.

The abstraction of arrays would be more useful if they permitted the index to take on many different dimensions. The nice thing in most languages is that they make it easy to specify arrays using multiple dimensions.

In a language like Java, you can simply declare different dimensions for an array in the following manner.

```
// define a new empty array of two dimensions
int[] example_1 = new int[9][7];

// define a new empty array of three dimensions
int[] example_2 = new int[9][7][6];

// Assign elements within an array
for (int i = 0; i < 9; i++) {
 for (int j = 0; j < 7; j++)
    example_1[i][j] = 9 * i + j;
}
```

The definition of the abstraction should now be updated to be:

Data Structure Name: Array
Constraints:
    (i) Collection has a fixed capacity along each dimension
    (ii) Collection has one or more dimensions
Operations:
    Create instance specifying number of dimensions and capacity along each dimension,
      store a record at index, retrieve record at index, delete record at index
Utility:
    Easy way to handle a collection of records via index along one or more dimensions

The implementation would need to be modified a little bit, and the index of any object needs to be mapped to a single dimension. One way to do this would be to convert a multi-dimensional index to a single-dimensional index. Suppose a multidimensional index is (i, j, k, l) and the capacity along each dimension is C_i, C_j, C_k and C_l respectively. The one-dimensional index would be $iC_i + jC_j + kC_k + lC_l$. We can also consider the general case of n dimensions where the multi-dimensional index is $x_1, x_2, x_3 \ldots x_n$ and the capacities are $C_1, C_2, C_3 \ldots C_n$ respectively. This can be mapped to a one-dimensional index such as $x_1C_1 + x_2C_2 + x_3C_3 + \ldots + x_nC_n$.

Performance

For the common types of operations that are performed, the following table lists the complexity of each operation for an array which has capacity *n*.

Operation	Runtime Complexity	Notes
create	O(constant)	
add	O(constant)	Requires index to be specified
search	O(n)	Needs comparing each existing data record in the array
remove	O(constant)	Assumes index is specified. If not, search needs to be performed to find index, which is O(n)
destroy	O(constant)	

Unlimited Capacity Array

An enhancement to the limited capacity array is to create an unlimited capacity array. This eliminates the challenge associated with remembering how much space is needed upfront. The array should increase in capacity as needed. The abstraction would look identical except for a reduction in the constraints of the abstraction.

Data Structure Name: Array
Constraints: None
Operations:
create instance, store a record at index, retrieve record at index, delete record at index
Utility:
Easy way to handle a collection of records via index, structure that grows as needed

---

The implementation of the structure can be done by maintaining a series of standard arrays with limited capacity. One can start with one array with a capacity of C. In case, a C+1th record is needed, one can create another array with the capacity of C.

In this case, items with index less than C are kept in the first array. Items with index between C and 2C are kept in the second array. Items with index between 2C and 3C are kept in the third array. The system can be continued to support an arbitrary number of arrays that are allocated on demand.

In an alternative implementation, one can also introduce a hierarchy of arrays. The top of the hierarchy would have C pointers to a set of arrays of capacity C. One such tier (as shown in Figure 14) can handle indices up to C^2. If needed another tier of hierarchy can be added to deal with even larger set of indices. Having K such tiers will result in an array that can have a capacity of CK. In this manner, almost an array with no constraints on indices can be supported.

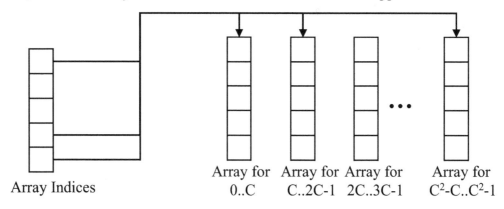

Array Indices   Array for   Array for   Array for   Array for
0..C   C..2C-1   2C..3C-1 C^2-C..C^2-1

Figure 14. One single tier for managing an unlimited capacity array

Application: Obfuscation by Rotation

Arrays are very useful in solving a variety of problems. In this section we look at some of the problems that can be solved using arrays. Our approach to solving these problems would be to define new abstractions, one in which the problem can be solved easily. When solving the problem, the abstraction construct allows us to solve the category of problems rather than just solving a specific instance of the problem.

Let us consider the problem of hiding the content of a message. In the early days of the Internet, people would post text-based messages on public discussion forums. There was a code of conduct in these forums that one would not post content unsuitable for minors on these forums. However, some people wanted to post material that were only intended for adults, and did not want to violate the code of conduct. A scheme called rot-13 was used by these people in which each character of the post was shifted by 13 characters forward in the English alphabet to create a scrambled version of the message. When somebody saw the garbled version, it was very apparent that the material was not suitable for minors. The reader could choose to skip the message or explicitly call rot-13 on the message which would unscramble the message.

Describing the process of rot-13 in more detail, let us look at the table shown in Figure 15, which shows the index for each of the 26 letters in the English alphabet from A-Z. It is common in computer science to start counting from 0 so the index ranges from 0 to 25. The second row in the table labeled "In" shows the corresponding letter at any index which is present in the alphabet. The third row labeled "Out" shows the letter when it is shifted by 13 positions.

Index	0	1	2	3	4	5	6	7	8	9	10	11	12	13	14	15	16	17	18	19	20	21	22	23	24	25
In	A	B	C	D	E	F	G	H	I	J	K	L	M	N	O	P	Q	R	S	T	U	V	W	X	Y	Z
Out	N	O	P	Q	R	S	T	U	V	W	X	Y	Z	A	B	C	D	E	F	G	H	I	J	K	L	M

Figure 15. Substitution Table for rot-13

When the input is a string such as 'let us get coffee' using the table above would translate the phrase to 'yrg hf trg pbssrr'. Since the alphabet consists of 26 letters, two rotations of 13 cancel each other out.

The obfuscation scheme is not limited to rotating by 13 characters. One can rotate the character by any other number, e.g. one can use rot-5 or rot-9. The scrambling requires shifting the character forward by the specific number of places. The unscrambling requires shifting the number backward by the specific number of places.

We want to implement an approach for general text obfuscation using rotation of letters. To solve this problem, we introduce an abstraction called the Obfuscator which is defined as below:

Abstraction Name: Obfuscator
Constraints:
    (i) Only modified input characters which are English capital alphabet characters
    (ii) Other characters need to be left unchanged
Operations:
    create with input of rotation distance, scramble plaintext input, unscramble a scrambled input,
Utility:
    Provides scrambling and unscrambling with arbitrary rotation distance

---

Having defined this abstraction, we explore an approach to implement it.

One way would be to create a system which contains two arrays of characters, each of capacity 26 characters. The first array would contain the characters of English alphabet shifted forward by the rotation distance. The second array would consist of characters shifted backward by the rotation distance. These two arrays can be created during the initialization of the obfuscator abstraction.

When an input string needs to be scrambled, one can consider the string character by character. The index of the character can be determined by seeing how far it is from the character 'A' (if upper case). Then the corresponding character at that index in the first array can be used to determine the obfuscated value of that character. Combining all the obfuscated characters will produce the scrambled string.

When unscrambling, the same approach is used except that the second array in the class is used to unscramble instead of the first.

The concrete implementation in Java corresponding to the approach described above is available at: https://github.com/dinesh-personal/data_structures/java/Chapter6.java.

Exercise 4.   Can you implement the same abstraction without using any arrays at all?

Exercise 5.   The current definition of Obfuscator only deals with capital letters in the alphabet, not the small letters. How would you extend the abstraction definition so that you can handle small letters which are included within the text?

Exercise 6.   The current definition of Obfuscator only deals with letters in the alphabet, not the numerals. How would you extend the abstraction definition so that you can handle numbers embedded within the text?

Application: Substitution Cipher

A scheme like rot-13 is good for a public forum where the sender is giving the choice to the readers whether or not they want to unscramble a message. However, there are many occasions when one wants to send a message to a targeted receiver and not have the message be visible to anyone other than the targeted receiver. One way to enable this secrecy is for the sender and the receiver have some shared knowledge which allows them (and only them) to understand what the intended message is.

One approach to obtain this goal is to use what is called a substitution cipher. In substitution cipher, each letter of the alphabet is replaced by another letter of the alphabet. In the cipher shown in Figure 15, there was a clear relationship between the in row and the out row with the shifting, and with up to 26 possible rotation distances, 26 possible different values of the out row can be generated. If instead of considering the shifts only, we consider that any mapping of the 26 letters to each other can be done, one can generate 26! different values of the out row, which basically consists of all permutations of the normal order of the alphabet.

The value of 26! is large, but not so large that it cannot be broken by modern computers. However, this does provide a rudimentary level of secrecy.

Substitution cipher can allow us to define a new abstraction, one which converts a plain message to a secret message and converts the secret message to the plain message. The abstraction would be defined as follows:

Abstraction Name: Encryptor
Constraints:
    (i) Operates only on input which has English alphabet characters
Operations:
    create with given substitution cipher table – generate a random one if none provided, encrypt plaintext input, decrypt encrypted input.
Utility:
    Provides encryption and decryption for any substitution cipher

The implementation of the substitution cipher would be done using an array which maintains the value to which each letter is mapped. At initialization table, the array needs to be provided. An example array would be:

| P | O | N | Q | T | S | R | W | U | V | Z | Y | X | A | B | F | G | H | C | D | E | J | I | M | L | K |

Using this array, A gets mapped to P, B gets mapped to O, C gets mapped to N and so on. When the plain text has to be encrypted, each letter is mapped to its corresponding value from the array. When the encrypted text has to be decrypted, the original letter corresponding to each character needs to be determined.

Instead of implementing the decryption using one array, an alternative approach is to maintain two arrays. One of the arrays is used for encryption and the other is used for decryption. This makes the implementation very similar to that used for rotation-based obfuscation described earlier.

Exercise 7.   The implementations of Encryptor and Obfuscator have significant functionality in common. How would you restructure the code of the two abstractions to reduce the redundancy in the code that is present?

Application: Operating System Cache

An Operating System (OS) is software written to simplify the task of using the computer hardware to its users. One of the benefits offered by the Operating System is to improve the performance of the computer when doing various tasks. The computer would contain of two types of storage systems – the non-volatile memory is storage that persists beyond power-cycles, and the volatile memory is storage that does not persist beyond power cycle. What it means is that the contents stored in the non-volatile storage are not lost when the computer is shut down, while volatile memory components are lost when the computer is shut down. Non-volatile storage is implemented using solid state drives (SSD) or hard drives. Volatile storage is offered by computer chips on the motherboard as referred to as main memory. Main memory is faster to access than the SSD, but generally has less storage capacity than the SSD.

One abstraction offered by the OS is a page – a fixed size segment of information maintained in the non-volatile memory/ One common task in OS is to retrieve pages from the non-volatile memory and make them available to the processor. Since main memory can be accessed faster than the non-volatile memory, the OS maintains a cache of frequently accessed pages in the main memory. When a page needs to be retrieved from the SSD, the OS first checks if it has it in the main memory and skips the task of retrieval in that case. This scheme is called caching.

Since main memory is generally smaller than SSD or hard disk, caches are limited to a fixed capacity corresponding to a small fraction of main memory. In a system where each page is 4 Kilobytes, and main memory is 4 Gigabytes, the main memory has the capacity of 10,48,576 pages. The system can reserve a cache of capacity 1024 pages without impacting other functions of the main memory significantly.

In an actual system, the amount of cache may differ depending on the nature of the workload that the system is optimized for. In some systems, you may want a larger amount of cache. In other systems which require very heavy use of memory, you may want a smaller amount of cache.

Following the abstraction-based approach, the initial step is to define an abstraction for the Cache.

We will define the following abstraction for the Cache

Abstraction Name: Cache
Constraints:
    (i) Can store up to capacity pages
Operations:
    create with capacity, search, insert,
Utility:
    Simplify the management of cache resources

Since the abstraction has fixed capacity, the array would be a logical choice to implement it. The array capacity is the size of the cache, and elements in the array are pages. Each page takes one entry in the array.

The OS cache can exist in one of the two states. Either it has less than its capacity (e.g. 1024) or it has reached its capacity. When the cache is not full, a new entry can be added to one of the available free locations in the cache. We do need a scheme to decide when the entry contains a valid page and when the entry is empty.

When the cache is full, and a new entry needs to be placed in the cache, the addition can not be done without discarding one of the existing entries. While many strategies to choose that entry can be used, we will simply use the approach that the oldest entry in the cache will be discarded. If the capacity is C, when new page C+1 is loaded, the page at index 0 is replaced. Note that when page C+2 is loaded, the page at index 1 should be replaced. The replacement is not exposed as an operation in the abstraction definition, so it should be done internally.

With this assumption, we can define a start location and an end location in the array which marks where the valid cache entries are. The start location points to the oldest entry in the cache and the end location points to the most recent entry in the cache. Since the end pointer will always be the start location plus the number of entries in the cache, we can choose to only keep the start pointer and the number of entries in the cache.

In the beginning, the start location and number of entries will both be set to 0. The end location is (start location plus the number of entries) modulo the capacity of the buffer. When the start and end pointer are the same, the cache has no entries.

When a new page needs to be added and the number of entries is less than the capacity of the array, it is put at the end location, and the number of entries incremented by 1. When the cache is full (i.e. the number of entries equals capacity), the page at start location is replaced with the new page, and start location incremented by 1.

Once this cache gets full to complete capacity, it will remain at full capacity and only the start pointer will continue to change.

Other Applications

In addition to the applications discussed earlier, arrays can be used for a variety of applications. These applications may include solving linear equations, handling matrix multiplication, and representing information. In games that are written using 2 or 3 dimensions of game space, arrays provide a convenient mechanism to monitor the state of the game. In artificial intelligence, it is usual to map any type of content into an array of numbers and then manipulate those arrays to make intelligent decisions.

Arrays are very ubiquitous, and we will use them in many different projects throughout the class.

Chapter Summary/Key Takeaways

An array is a very common and useful data structure. It allows storage and retrieval of data records using an index which can be one or more dimensions. Arrays can be used for a variety of applications within software development.

In the next chapter, we will look at the list data structure.

Chapter 7. Lists, Stacks and Queues

The list, just like array is a very common data structure. As discussed earlier, the list data structure is inspired from the various lists we maintain in real-life. Stacks and Queues are special types of lists which are used in many different applications.

Definition of Lists

A list is an unordered sequence of data records. Data records can be added to the list or removed from the list. It can be described by the following abstraction description:

Abstraction Name: List
Constraints:
   (i) provides an unlimited number of records in the list.
Operations:
    create, add, remove, search
Utility:
    Provides a convenient data structure used to build many further abstractions

Implementation of Lists

A list may be implemented in a variety of ways, but the easier way to implement would be to incorporate the concept of a pointer. A pointer is an abstraction that allows one to access a data record. For a data record, the pointer usually is the address of the data record in the memory of the computer.

The implementation of a list would maintain a pointer to the first item in the list. In some cases, one may also want to maintain a pointer to the last item in the list. The basic data record that is provided in the operations of the list data structure is converted into an enhanced data record that contains either one or two pointers. The former enables a singly linked list while the latter enables a doubly linked list.

The implementation of a list would maintain a pointer to the first element in the list. We can refer to this element as the head of the list. Each element in a singly linked list will point to the next element in the list.

Each element in a doubly linked list maintains pointers to the element before it and the element after it in the list. In doubly linked lists, one maintains a pointer to both the head of the list as well as the tail of the list. The pointer can be implemented as the memory location of the data record, with the value being zero (also called nil or null in some languages) if it is empty.

Insertion of a new data record can be done either at the head, the tail or somewhere in between the list. If the data record is inserted in the middle, either the data record before which it is inserted or the data record after which it would be inserted ought to be provided.

To insert a record at the head, the head will be pointed to the new record, and the next element of the head would be set to point to the original head in the list. If it is a doubly linked list, the previous pointer of the original head would be updated to point to the new head.

To insert a record at the tail, the tail would be updated to the new record, and the next pointer of the original tail will point to the new record. If it is a doubly linked list, the previous pointer of the new tail should be updated to point to the old tail as well.

To insert a data record N in between an item A and B, the next pointers of A would be updated to N, and the next pointer of N would be set to B. In case of doubly linked list, the previous pointer of B would be updated to N and the previous pointer of N would be updated to be B.

To search for an existing data record, the list is traversed from the beginning to the end comparing the item in the list to the item being searched. If an item is not found, the search results nothing. If a match is found, the corresponding record is returned.

Checking if a list is empty can be done by keeping track of number of data records in the list, incrementing the item every time a data record is added, and decrementing this value every time a data record is removed.

Performance

For the common types of operations that are performed, the following table lists the complexity of each operation for a list which has capacity *n*.

Operation	Runtime Complexity	Notes
isempty	O(constant)	This assumes the number of elements in list is tracked
add	O(constant)	Can be added at the head or tail or in middle with neighbors provided as parameters
search	O(n)	Needs comparing each existing data record in the array
remove	O(n)	Needs to perform a search to determine if element is present

This table is also valid for stacks, queues and other variants of lists that are discussed in this chapter.

Combined Data Structure: Limited Capacity List

While lists are generally assumed to have unlimited capacity, one can also define an abstraction which is a list with limited capacity. In all other respects, the limited capacity list provides the same operations as the capacity of the list. Since the list has limited capacity, it must support an operation that tells whether the list is full, i.e. at capacity.

While it may sound strange to restrict the capabilities of a list, a capacity constraint might make it easier to support some applications. If an application requires maintaining an upper limit on some type of records to maintain efficiency, a limited capacity list may be useful.

The limited capacity link would have the following definition

---

Abstraction Name: Limited Capacity List
Constraints:
   (i) provides up to the capacity limit data records in a list
   (ii) returns an error when one tries to add a record beyond capacity
Operations:
    create, add, remove, search, check if full
Utility:
    Prevents lists from growing too big

An implementation of the limited capacity list may be done by tracking the current number of entries in the list. Checking if the list is full is simply comparing the current number of entries and whether it equals the capacity. If the add operation is called when the list is full, an error is returned.

Stacks

A stack is a special type of data structure which follows the last-in first-out principle for adding and removing data records. This abstraction is defined as follows:

Abstraction Name: Stack
Constraints:
   (i) item put last in the list should be the first one to be popped
Operations:
    create, pop, push, search, peek, isempty
Utility:
    Supports a customized list with selected order of removing and adding data records

---

The push operation is an alias for add, and the pop operation as alias for remove. The peek operation allows one to look at the item at the top of the stack without removing it. The peek operation can be useful for manipulating stacks. In some cases, the pop operation may be called the poll operation.

From an implementation perspective, the stack simply implements the list structure but ensures that the add (push) operation only adds data records to the head of the list and the remove (pop) operation removes the item to the head of the list.

The need for stacks arises in many applications with some prominent ones being the support for function calling within various operating systems, as well as parsing of mathematical operations.

Queues

A queue is a data structure in which the first in first out principle for adding and removing data records is followed. This abstraction is defined as follows:

Abstraction Name: Queue
Constraints:
   (i) item enqueued last in the list should be the first one to be dequeued
Operations:
   create, pop, push, search, peek, isempty
Utility:
   Supports a customized list with selected order of removing and adding data records

The push operation is an alias for add, and the pop operation as alias for remove. The peek operation allows one to look at the item at the top of the stack without removing it. The peek operation can be useful for manipulating stacks.

From an implementation perspective, the stack simply implements the list structure but ensures that the add (push) operation only adds data records to the head of the list and the remove (pop) operation removes the item to the head of the list.

The need for queues arises in many applications with some prominent ones being the support for function calling within various operating systems, and the parsing of mathematical operations.

Exercise 8. A special type of queue is a priority queue. It is a queue in which the items being added are provided a priority which is a number. When removing items from the priority queue, the current member with highest priority is implemented. How would you define and implement the priority queue abstraction.

Application: Hangman Game

Hangman is a popular game in which the intention is to guess a word in 6 or less attempts. The computer uses a randomly used word as the answer and asks the user to guess for a letter in the word. If the user is able to guess a correct letter in the word, the user wins. At each attempt, a figure of a man being hanged is drawn, which goes through the sequences shown in Figure 16 at each failed attempt:

Figure 16. Sequence of images in the classic hangman game

In order to implement this game, we will have to create an abstraction of Game which can be defined as follows:

Abstraction Name: HangMan
Constraints:
   (i) Should not allow more than 6 attempts for guess
Operations:
   guess
Utility:
   Provides a useful way to pass time

To implement this abstraction, we need to maintain the state of the game. The state of the game consists of the right answer, the list of letters entered so far, and the number of attempts. To play the game, the computer will select a random word from a set of possible answers (e.g. a list of animal names). On each guess, the computer will update the list of letters entered, the number of attempts, and display the current figure of hangman if the word has not been guessed completely. The victory or failed message can be given as appropriate for the outcome of the game.

The complete code is available at:
https://github.com/dinesh-personal/data_structures/java/Chapter11.java.

Application: Check Out Counter Simulation

We can use a combination of the data structures we have learnt to solve some interesting real-world problem. Here is a problem that the manager of a grocery store may face.

The grocery store has customers coming in at different rates during different times of the day. The manager monitored the customers and checkout clerks and noted that:

- During the evenings, customers arrive randomly with the time-interval between two arriving customers ranging from 0 seconds (customers arrive at the same time) to 120 seconds. The arrival is uniformly distributed, and average is 60 seconds between two customers.

- During daytime, customers arrive randomly with the time-interval between two arriving customers ranging from 0 seconds (customers arrive at the same time) to 600 seconds. The arrival is uniformly distributed, and average is 300 seconds between two customers.

- The time to check out a customer at a checkout lane takes a minimum of 100 seconds and a maximum of 300 seconds with the average being 200 seconds.

- At most 10 counters can be open in the store.

If the manager does not want any customer to wait more than 120 seconds to start the checkout process, how many checkout counters should the manager open during evening hours and during daytime. The manager wants to open as few counters as possible while satisfying this constraint.

Note that we need to solve the same problem twice, so we should think in terms of the abstractions that can solve the problem given the input maximum, minimum and average separation between arrival of customers. We would start by defining the abstraction that we would like to have:

Abstraction Name: Check Out Planner
Constraints:
   (i) calc_counters should return an integer value between 1 and 10
Operations:
    creation – specifies customer arrival rate and check out time
    calc_counters – returns number of counters to meet an upper bound on customer wait time
Utility:
    helps identify the top level capability to solve the problem

---

The creation of this abstraction takes the following inputs:

- Customer arrival rate – in number of customers per hour

- Checkout time of customers – in number of minutes per customer

The calc_counters operation takes the following inputs:

- Maximum customer wait time objective - in minutes
and returns

- The number of counters to open

We need to figure out how we will implement this operation. One way to solve this problem is to run through the scenario with an increasing number of check-out counters, i.e. 1 counter, 2 counters, 3 counters etc. and see what the resulting customer wait time would be. If it is less than the objective, we can return the number. If it is more than the objective, we will check with an increased number of counters. Note that this approach is an example of brute force enumeration that we discuss in Chapter 10.

In order to use this approach, we need another abstraction which would assume that the number of counters, the checkout time and customer arrival rate are given, and return us the wait time of the customers. The challenge we face is that the answer depends on the way the customers arrive and are serviced, and each customer arrival and service is random.

One approach to overcome the randomness challenge is to run through several scenarios under which customer arrive and are serviced according to the specifications we have been provided. Each scenario could run through 4 hours of the operation of the store, which would be the typical evening rush hour. We could use the computer to run through 1000 such scenarios and take the average of the wait time to estimate the wait time of the customer.

In other words, we need to define two other abstractions which can be defined as follows:

Abstraction Name: Averager
Constraints:
    (i) average only deals with numeric values
Operations:
      report – report one single value to be used in the average
      average – returns the average delay from all the reported values

---

The aggregator task is to average the results, so we will simply define it to have two operations, one to pass the results of a simulation and the other to average out the results.

Abstraction Name: Simulation
Constraints:
    (i) calc_counters should return an integer value between 1 and 10
Operations:
      estimate – estimate the wait time given customer arrival times, service times, number of counters, and number of hours to simulate.

Note that for these two abstractions, we are skipping the utility statement since the obvious utility is that of solving the problem.

To implement the Simulation abstraction, we need another two abstractions, one for the Customer and one for a Checkout Clerk. Each Customer has an arrival time, and a wait time before the customer is serviced. Each clerk is either free or busy, and if busy becomes free at some time.

The simulation process for implementing estimate operation with these two abstractions is relatively straightforward. We start from a starting time of 0 seconds and check what happens at every second interval. When a customer arrives, it is put into a queue. When a clerk is free at some time, it services the customer and updates its status and the time when the service is done. The process is repeated till four hours are simulated.

Complete code is at https://github.com/dinesh-personal/data_structures/java/Chapter11.java.

Queues and lists can be used to simulate other real-world scenarios just like this situation.

Chapter Summary/Key Takeaways

List provide data structure which maintains multiple data records. Special lists such as queues and stacks enforce addition and remove of data records. Lists can be implemented with or without a bound on the number of data records. They can be useful in many different problems where the initial number of elements are not always easy to determine upfront.

In the next chapter, we look at the tree data structure.

Chapter 8.   Trees

A tree data structure maintains information in a hierarchy of parents and children. The tree is composed of component abstractions called nodes. Nodes have the relationship of parent and children among themselves. If node A is a parent of node B, then node B is a child of node A. A node with no parent is called the root node. Each tree can have at most one root node. A node with no children is called a leaf. A node which is neither a leaf nor the root is called an inner node.

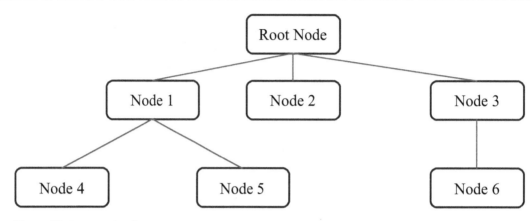

Figure 17. An example of a tree

Figure 17 shows an example of a tree. Node 1, Node 2 and Node 3 are children of the root node. Node 4, Node 5 and Node 6 are leaf nodes. Node 3 is a parent of Node 6, and Node 6 is the child of Node 3.

In the tree, there is always one and only one path between the root node and any other node. Any node that lies along this path is called an ancestor of the node at the end of the path. The root node is an ancestor of all the nodes in the tree. Conversely, the node at the end of the path will be called a descendent of the nodes that lie along the path from the root. All nodes are descendants of the root node. The children of any node are generally arranged in an order ranging from left-most child to the right-most child.

The number of children of a node is called its degree. A leaf node has a degree of 0. Any non-leaf node has a degree of 1 or more. If each node in the tree (except the leaf nodes) have the same degree, the tree is called a k-ary tree. A tree where each non-leaf node has a degree of 2 is called a binary tree. If each leaf node in the tree has the same depth, the tree is called a balanced tree.

The number of links it takes to reach from the root to a node is called its depth. The alternative name of the depth is level of a node. Each node has a unique depth or level.

The solution of many types of problems requires traversing all nodes in the tree. This traversal can be done in a few different ways. The traversal of the tree results in listing out all the trees in the node in a specific order. The following are some of the common ways in which trees are traversed:

- Pre-order: The root is listed first. Then the subtrees formed by the children are traversed in pre-order from left to right.

- In-order: The subtree formed by the left-most child of the root is traversed in the order from left to right. Then the root is listed. Then the subtrees formed by other children of the root are traversed in-order from the second left-most child to the right-most child.

- Post-Order: The subtrees formed by the children of the tree are traversed in the order from left to right. Then the root node is listed.

- Breath-first: The root (with depth 0) is listed first. Then all the nodes with depth 1 are listed. Then all the nodes with depth 2 are listed, and so on until all the nodes have been listed.

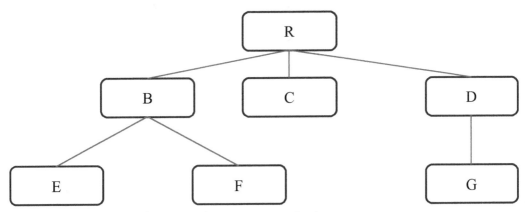

Figure 18. A sample tree to demonstrate the various traversal orders

For the tree shown in Figure 18, the various traversal orders will be as follows:

- Pre-Order: **R**, B, E, F, C, D, G

- In-Order: E, B, F, **R**, C, D, G

- Post-Order: E, F, B, C, G, D, **R**

- Breadth-First: **R**, B, C, D, E, F, G

You may find the definition of tree traversal order to be somewhat unusual. The definition is being done recursively, i.e. done by calling the term being defined within itself. This trick, called recursion, is very useful in solving a variety of problems, and is one of the common problem-solving approaches that is used widely in computer science. In practice, it means that a function would call itself. More details are discussed in Chapter 11.

The traversal of a tree is converting data maintained as a tree into a list and is an example of the transformation of one type of data structure into another type. Information maintained in a tree structure can be converted to a list structure using any of the traversal approaches, and conversely one can write a routine which takes in data maintained as a list and convert it to a tree structure, using the traversal order as another input for the conversion process.

We are now ready to define the tree abstraction as:

Abstraction Name: Tree
Constraints:
    (i) data records are put into a parent-child hierarchy with other data records
    (ii) There is only one unique path between the root node and any other node in the tree
Operations:
    create, insert, remove, search, traverse
Utility:
    Uses the hierarchy to improve the search capability of data records

---

Given the definition of the tree and its various orders of traversal, you may want to consider a few sample exercises. You may want to use your access to GenAI tools to write the following program:

Exercise 9.   Write a program that converts a listing of nodes in a tree from one order of traversal to another order. The program will take an input list with the names of the nodes, the order of the traversal for the input list, and the order of the traversal for the output list. It should output a list of nodes.

Searching in Trees

The primary benefit of trees is that they allow one to search through the data records maintained in the data structure very efficiently. This allows for a much faster search of the content of the data records compared to the array or the list. When information is maintained in a list, one needs to examine every item in the list to check whether the item is present or not. When information is maintained in an array without any order, searching requires traversing all the data records in the array. One can organize the structure to search through an array more efficiently, but in effect the approach relies on approaches to implement a tree-like data structure within an array. What it means is that the search through a list or an unsorted array is $O(n)$ if the data structure has n data records.

One approach for searching would be to traverse all the nodes in any one of the traversal order and check whether the data being searched for is present. However, this will still be $O(n)$. However, one can use the left-right relationship among the children of any node to do an efficient search. Searching requires that data records be comparable, i.e. we can take two data records and determine which one is smaller or larger among the two, or whether the two are equal.

The basic trick is to ensure that the data record maintained at each subtree of a node have an ordering relationship among each other. Suppose we can ensure that a child to the left is always smaller than the data record maintained in a child to the right. We can then use this relationship to determine which of the subtrees of the children would have the data record we are searching for.

If we can structure the data so that we only have to follow one of the subtrees within the tree, we will only be following the path from the root to one of the leaf nodes to determine whether or not the data record is present in the tree. The process may best be illustrated by means of an example. Suppose we need to search through a list of names of animals – Ant, Ape, Bat, Bee, Cat, Cod, Cow, Dog, Eel, Emu, Fox, Hen, Owl, Pig, Rat, Yak.

To search efficiently through these names, we will create a search tree as follows: The children of root will be the unique set of first letters in the list of names. These are nodes with depth 1. The children of a node with depth 2 will be the unique set of first 2 letters in the list of names where the first letter matches the node. The children of a node with depth 3 will be the unique set of first 3 letters in the list of names which has the first 2 letters matching the node. Each child shares the prefix of its parents and adds one more letter for its content. The resulting tree is as shown in Figure 19

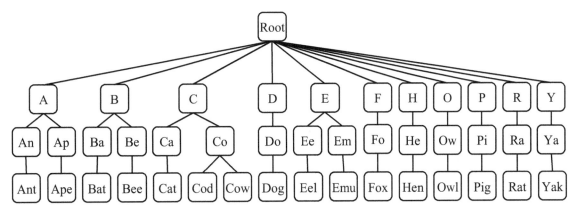

Figure 19. Example Search Tree

To search for any string in the list of names in this tree, we can take the first character in the string and check if it matches any of the children of the root node. Then we take the first two characters in the name and check which child of the node matches them. We repeat the same comparison for the next level. If the word is found in the tree, we will be able to reach the matching word at the leaf in exactly 3 node traversals.

Any child of the node would only have at most 26 children, so at any node the comparison time will be bounded by a constant – the time take to compare 26 strings. The amount of time we will make the comparison is limited by the tree which is bounded by the maximum length of any string in the set.

In this simple example, it may look like we are making too many comparisons compared to simply comparing against all the lists. However, if there were a large number of words, e.g. ten million words that we are searching against, the organization in the tree would result in a much faster search than comparing against all the words.

If the tree were regular k-ary tree and h levels deep, it would have k^h leaves at the bottom most level, and any path will only be h level deep. In other words, a search process in a tree would only take h steps instead of k^h steps. If the tree has n nodes, the search process would be $O(\log n)$. This can offer a significant speed-up in the process of searching for entries in a collection.

The scheme we used for organizing the nodes in Figure 19 is not the only one that can be used. One obvious optimization is to delete a node which has only one child to reduce the number of nodes. This will result in a much simpler tree.

Performance

For the common types of operations that are performed, the following table lists the complexity of each operation for a tree which has *n* entries.

Operation	Runtime Complexity	Notes
isempty	O(constant)	This assumes the number of elements in tree is tracked
Add	See notes	O(log n) – if its parent node needs to be determined O(constant) – if its parent node is specified
Search	O(log n)	Assumes that the data is organized properly
Remove	See notes	O(constant) – if removed without modifying the other nodes
Traverse	O(n)	Regardless of order, all nodes need to be examined once

The performance chart depends on the structure of the tree. If the data within the tree is not organized properly, search can take O(n) time. At the same time, reorganizing the tree when nodes are added or removed can cause significant number of operations.

Application: Decision Automation

In various applications, software needs to make decisions regarding what action to take next. An example would be a computer playing a game like chess. The computer needs to decide what move to make in response to the actions made by another player. Similarly, when computer software is used to decide issues like whether to approve or reject a loan application, or whether a new device detected on the network is a computing device (e.g. laptop, mobile phone or computer) or an IoT device (a thermostat, controller for an elevator etc.), a decision tree can help make this decision.

A sample decision tree used to make decisions on loan applications is shown in Figure 20. The decision process starts by looking at the FICO score of the applicant. The FICO score is an credit-worthiness score created originally by the **Fair Isaac Corporation** which is now used widely within the financial industry. The score ranges to a maximum of 850, with the higher score indicating an individual who has low risk of defaulting on a loan. The debt ratio of an applicant is the monthly obligation payments of the applicant divided by the monthly income of the applicant. The lower the debt ratio, the more money the applicant has.

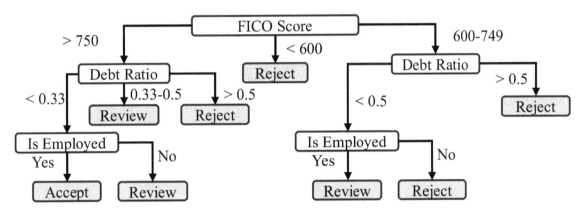

Figure 20. An exemplar decision tree used for deciding on loan applications

For the particular decision tree ratio, the bank making the loan can automatically reject or accept some applications and requires manual review of others. If the applicant FICO score is high (over 750), the debt ratio including this loan is less than 0.33 and the applicant is employed, the application is automatically accepted. If the FICO score is low (below 600), the applicant is automatically rejected. Applicants with high debt ratio (over 0.5) are also automatically rejected. Applicants with medium FICO scores (600-749) who have a low debt ratio (< 0.5) are reviewed if they are employed, otherwise rejected.

The decision tree can be used to reduce the number of loan applications which require manual review by the bank staff. The use of decision trees in other applications where decisions are to be made can significantly improve automation and reduce the burden on individuals.

Chapter Summary/Key Takeaways

Trees provide an efficient organization of data which can help searching through information more efficiently, e.g. in $O(\log n)$ steps instead of $O(n)$ steps. They are used in a wide variety of information processing, data storage, file system representation and multiple other use-cases.

In the next chapter, we take a look at the hash-set data structure.

Chapter 9. Maps and Hash Tables

A map is a data structure that allows for an efficient indexing of data records using a key. The data record in this case is also known as a value, and maps can be viewed as a scheme to maintain a key-value pairing. For the scope of this chapter, any reference to the value is the references to the data record maintained within the data structure.

The general concept of a map can be illustrated by means of a library catalogue. Each book maintained in the library has a location on one of the stacks in the library. Given a title of a book, it is frequent operation to find the location of the book. A map structure can be used to lookup the location. Of course, the title can also be used to look up other attributes of the book, e.g. its author, its subject, whether it has been lent out to someone, and when it is expected back.

Because of the use of the key, the add and remove operations within a map are slightly different than that of the other data structures. The addition and removal operation require the key to be specified. Adding a data record using a key is generally referred to as the put operation, and retrieving the data record using the key is referred to as the get operation. Because of the use of keys and values construct, maps are also known as key-value pairs, k-v pairs, key-value maps, and k-v maps.

Here is the definition of a map abstraction:

Data Structure Name: Map
Constraints:
   (i) Index can be any arbitrary data type
Operations:
   create instance, put record with key, get record with key, delete record with key, search
Utility:
   Easy way to handle a collection of records via index of arbitrary type

---

Implementation as Hash Tables

One way to implement a map can be envisioned using arrays. One can store each data record in an array. The array contains both the key and the value (data record). When a get operations happened, one searches through the array to find the matching key and on a match return the associated value. The search will take the amount of time it takes for the search in the array to happen. Instead of an array, a list can also be used with the same logic.

This implementation is inefficient, and a significant speedup can be obtained by using a hash-function. Instead of placing the key-value pairs at any location in the array, the location is determined by the key. If an array of size C is being used to store the data records, a function is used to compute a location for any key. This function for computing location from key should yield a location less than C for any key. The function which computes the location is called the hash-function, and the result is called the hash of the key.

Hashes can be computed in many ways. If the key is a single character, the hash could be the binary representation of that character modulo the size of the array. Alternatively, the hash for an alphanumerical key could be the difference between its Unicode value and the Unicode value of 'A'. If a key is a string, one can add all the code representations of the individual characters and take the sum modulo the size of the array as the hash. In some cases, the hash can be obtained by looking at the binary representation of the key and selecting a subset of bits in this representation as representing the hash.

In some cases, the hash function of two different keys can be the same. This means that the values corresponding to those keys would be stored in the same location. This is called a collision in the keys, and can be handled in two ways:

- Have the array at that location point to a list which contains the keys and the values in each data record.

- Store the key-value pair at the next free location in the array which is not occupied.

The former requires searching through the list on a get command, and the latter requires searching through the subsequent entries of an array. Both are undesirable and a good hash function should not have too many collisions. An ideal hash function would have no collisions.

The resulting structure is called a hash-table since it stored values at locations determined by a hash of the keys. With a well-designed hash function, the get and put operation in a map can be done in O(constant) time.

> **Exercise 10.** Access the GenAI tool that you have access to and ask it to list out some of the common hash functions.

Performance

The performance of the hash table depends on the number of collisions that happen during the hashing process. The number of collisions depends both on the hash function that is selected and the set of keys that are being hashed. As a result, the performance would have two components – the run time expected in the average case where there are few collisions, and the run-time expected in the worst case where we keep on having collisions after collisions.

The following table lists the complexity of each operation for a map which has n entries with both the best-case complexity as well as the worst-case complexity. The worst-case complexity will be O(n) in all cases since the hash function may be unfortunate enough to go into a behavior where every operation results in a hash collision:

Operation	Average Runtime Complexity	Worst Runtime Complexity
put	O(constant)	O(n)
get	O(constant)	O(n)
Remove	O(constant)	O(n)

The Set Data Structure

A set is a collection of records in which there are no duplicate entries. A set data structure can be defined as follows:

> **Data Structure Name:** Set
> **Constraints:**
>   (i) No key should occur more than once in the data structure
> **Operations:**
>   create instance, add record, search, delete record
> **Utility:**
>   Easy way to handle a collection of records with unique keys.

When an add operation is asked for a key that is present already, the data structure definition ought to determine its behavior – whether an error should be signaled or the addition operation ignored. Let us assume for now that adding an existing record is ignored.

A set can be implemented with as a list or a hash-map as the basic underlying data structure. When implemented as a list, the add operation ought to check that the entry does not already exist. It can be done in two steps, check for existing key and insert if the check shows the key does not exist. The same logic applies for implementing sets using hash-maps. On an add operation, the search should be done, and the put on the hash-map called only if the record does not already exist.

> **Exercise 11.**   Implement the set data structure using both the list and hash-set as the underlying implementation. What would be the O-complexity of adding, searching and deleting in both implementations.

Application: Word Frequency Count

Let us consider the problem where we are given a list of words, and we want to count the number of words that start with a given character from A-Z. We can represent that as a key-value pair where the keys are the letters in the alphabet from A-Z and the value is the count of the words beginning with the key.

70

A map is a convenient data structure to do this counting. Define a map which is indexed by the key containing single letter of the alphabet. The value for all 26 letters of the alphabet is set to be 0. Then we can go through the list of names, pick the first letter as the key, and increment the value stored in the map for the key.

Following the paradigm for defining abstractions, we can define the abstraction for frequency counter as:

Data Structure Name: FrquencyCounter
Constraints:
    (i) Inputs have to be valid strings in the programming language
Operations:
    create instance, count a string, populate with many strings, print out
Utility:
    Simple frequency counter by first character in the string

---

The Java code for the same can be found at https://github.com/dinesh-personal/data_structures/java/Chapter9.java.

In a general case, we may want to count the word frequency not just for the initial character but for a set of initial prefixes, e.g. the frequency count using the first two characters in the string. The same code will work except that our key is a string consisting of the first two characters in the alphabet. However, since we will have to initialize 26*26 key-value pairs, and most of the keys will not have any strings, the initialization will be relatively expensive.

We can improve the efficiency of the algorithm by not initializing the key-values at the beginning but checking if a key exists in the map before updating it. If the key does not exist, that value is initialized to 1. This results in a map with a smaller number of entries.

Data Structure Name: FrquencyCounter2
Constraints:
    (i) Inputs have to be valid strings in the programming language
Operations:
    create instance, count a string, populate with many strings, print out
Utility:
    Simple frequency counter by first two characters in the string

---

The Java code for the same can be found at https://github.com/dinesh-personal/data_structures/java/Chapter9.java.

Application: Content Caching

Many algorithms in computer science depend on making a request to a service and receiving a response from the service. Often time, the service is slow or may be expensive to respond. If the same set of requests are made multiple time to the service, then the latency of accessing the service can be reduced by checking if a request has been made recently and returning the previous response if the check succeeds.

This scheme can be implemented by maintaining two maps, each using the request as the key. The first map stores the time when the request was made, and the second map stores the response which was returned. When future requests are received, the map checks if the request is present in the first map. A request is made to the service if one of these following conditions hold true:

- The key is not present in the first map

- The key is present in the map, but the value stored in the first map is less than the current time minus a specified threshold.

If neither of the two conditions are satisfied, the response stored corresponding to the request in the second map is returned.

When a request to the service is made, the current time when the response was received is stored in the first map and the returned response is stored in the second map.

A similar scheme can be used with a single map by defining the value as a data record consisting of two attributes – the time when the response was received and the actual response.

Chapter Summary/Key Takeaways

Maps provide a convenient way to take any type of data structure and look up data records associated with it. They are also known as the key-value pairs. They are implemented using hash-tables using a hash-function to map the key to an index in an array where the data record is stored.

This marks the last chapter of this section. In the next section, we will examine some of the applications that can be developed using various data structures.

Part III. Common Problems Solved with Data Structures

Having gone through the basic abstractions of some of the data structures, let us examine some of the common problems that can be solved using the data structures we have learnt about.

In the first chapter of this section, we review some of the common approaches to solve problems in computer science.

The next chapter delves into the subject of recursion and how that simplifies the writing of many of the common programming approaches.

The subsequent chapter discusses the problem of searching through a set of records and how the process can be improved using various data structures.

The following chapter discusses the task of sorting a set of data records in ascending or descending order.

The final chapter in the book includes some software development exercises that the student can undertake to use and exploit the various data structures and approaches to solve problems in computer science.

Chapter 10. Common Problem-Solving Techniques

The goal of learning about data structures is to solve problems in software development that we may face some day. Over the years of solving problems with software, several useful techniques have been developed. It is useful to briefly review some of those schemes.

Brute Force Enumeration

In many situations we are asked to solve a problem for which there are a finite possibility of solutions. The problem may be hard to solve directly, but one can run through all the finite potential solutions and check if they solve the problem.

We can consider the following problem: write a program which takes four inputs a, b, c and d and finds the smallest value of x which is less than 100 and satisfied the constraint $ax^3+bx^2+cx=d$. The solution may or may not exist.

It may not always be easy to solve a cubic equation, but we know that there are only 100 possible solutions from 0 to 99. While it may be tedious for a human to check all the 100 possible solutions, it would be trivial for a computer to try out all the values and see which one satisfies the value. If we run through all the possible solutions starting from 0, we will find one that satisfies the cubic or reach the limit of 99. The first solution that satisfies the cubic is the right answer.

Another problem that can be solved using brute force enumeration is the following. We are given a plain-text string and an encrypted version of the same string. We know that the algorithm used for encryption is rot-x where each character is rotated forward by x characters. We want to determine what the rotation is.

In this situation, there are only 26 possible answers. Therefore, it makes sense to run through all the possibilities and then check which among the 26 is the right answer.

While brute-force enumeration may not be the most elegant or impressive among the various strategies to solve the solution, it is very effective for solving a class of problems.

Divide and Conquer

The principle of divide and conquer is borrowed from an eponymous phrase 'divide and rule' in politics used by several empires. The basic idea is that while governing a large empire is a difficult process, dividing it into smaller groups to administer makes the task easier. In politics, the division often happens along ethnic or demographic boundaries and the practice is not advisable. In computer science, the division into smaller problems is done on technical grounds and the practice of divide and conquer, where appropriate, can be very useful.

An example of divide and conquer can be seen in the bisection-based solution of equations using numeric analysis method. Suppose you are given the task of finding the values of x which solve the $f(x) = 0$. The assumption is that the function is continuous in the interval in which we are looking for the solution. We start by taking two guesses for the values of x, say *a* and *b* which have the values of *f(a)* and *f(b)* with opposite signs, i.e. if *f(a)* is positive *f(b)* is negative and if *f(a)* is negative then *f(b)* must be positive.

If the function is continuous, positive on one side and negative on the other side, it must become zero at one or more points in between them. The divide and conquer approach would try to simplify the problem by dividing the region over which the answer is to be found into smaller ones. The bisection method looks at the value of the function mid-point between *a* and *b*. Depending on the sign of the function at this mid-point, one or the other half of the region is selected. The process can then be repeated on this smaller interval.

The repetition of the bisection of the region results in the system converging towards one of the regions where the function would be close to 0. By repeatedly dividing the search region into half, an effective solution can be obtained rapidly.

Greedy Algorithm

Many problems in computer science require a solution which requires selecting either once or repeated time. For example, when an Operating System finds its processor to be free, it needs to select which among one or more processes that are ready to be executed ought to be done. Since the best selection may not depend just on the current set of ready processes but also on some of the processes that may imminently become ready, the processor needs to determine whether to select a process immediately or to wait for some time. The greedy algorithm is an approach which will select the best choice based on the current information, rather than wait for a more complex evaluation.

It is possible that an algorithm that can anticipate and predict future tasks that will get ready shortly to determine which process to run next. If a very high priority process will be getting ready in imminent future, it may be worthwhile waiting for that task to become ready or to schedule a process that will complete just before the high priority process comes ready.

In some cases, the greedy approach produces an optimal solution. If each of the processes that are ready to run have an estimated time to completion, picking the shortest job first produces an optimal scheme for minimizing the average time jobs finish in. If each of the processes that are ready to run have a deadline to be completed by, the greedy approach for picking the job with the earliest deadline minimizes the percentage of jobs that miss their deadlines.

The big benefit of a greedy approach is the speed at which decisions can be made, even if it not always optimal. This makes the greedy approach a good heuristic to solve problems that may require complex computation to make an optimal decision.

Backtracking

Backtracking is an effective technique to solve problems where a solution satisfying some constraints has to be found. Backtracking is good to solve puzzles like Sudoku or crossword problems.

Backtracking works by finding a partial candidate solution which satisfies the constraints that are provided for the problem. It then tries to extend the partial candidate solution and checks if the extension can solve the problem. If an extension fails to solve the problem, the algorithm backtracks and tries to extend the problem another way.

The general algorithm can be seen as an attempt to build a tree data structure where the root of the tree contains the initial partial candidate solution. Each node in the tree contains a candidate solution (partial for inner nodes, complete for the leaf nodes) which is an extension of the partial candidate solution at its parent node. Backtracking tries to do a depth-first search of this tree giving up on the partial solution which violates the constraint and are thus not viable.

To illustrate the process, let us consider a classical problem - the 8-queens problem. The problem asks for placing 8 queens on a standard chess board of 8x8 such that no pair of queens can attack each other. By the definition of the problem, every row and column on the board can have only one queen piece on it. The initial partial candidate solution is one in which no queens are placed on the board. The next extension of this partial solution can be used by placing one queen on one of the 8 possible columns on row 0. Next, extensions of this solution which try to place a queen on each of the 8 possible columns on row 1 are tried. The locations where the two queens attack each other are discarded and the next one tried. When a location on row 2 that does not conflict with the previous two is found, the location on row 3 are searched for, and so on.

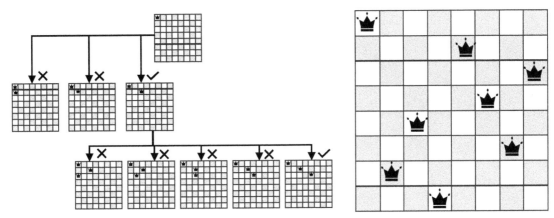

Figure 21. The 8-queens problem initial steps for backtracking and one of the final solutions

The initial step of the algorithm along with the complete solution is shown in Figure 21. The search starts from the first row and first column as shown in the top of the tree shown on the left of the figure. After which two columns in the second row are discarded (shown with a x) but the third column results in a solution where the two queens do not attack each other. This is shown with a check mark. After finding one partial solution that satisfies the constraint with 2 queens, the position of the 3rd queen is determined on the third row. Here four attempts shown with a cross fail, but the fifth one succeeds. At the next step the fourth queen position will be tried (this step is not shown). The resulting solution after all the steps complete is shown on the right-hand side of the figure.

Effectively, the entire enumeration of all possible combinations is being made by following a tree, but any non-viable solution is discarded quickly so that the traversal of the partial solution tree can be done in an efficient manner.

Chapter Summary/Key Takeaways

In this chapter we looked at some of the common problem-solving techniques that can be sued to develop software and address specific problems at hand. Specific topics covered include brute-force enumeration, divide and conquer, greedy approach and backtracking. While these are not the only way to solve problems, these cover a broad segment of interesting problems.

In the next chapter, we take a look at recursion which is a common technique to implement most of these problem-solving techniques.

Chapter 11. Recursion

Recursion is a convenient technique that makes the implementation of many types of problem-solving techniques easier.

The basic problem-solving approach consists of calling functions or subroutines as we implement a software-based solution to the problem. In general, a function implementation can call other functions that are defined. In recursion, the function calls itself during its definition.

When the function calls itself, it runs a danger that it may call itself an infinite number of times. To avoid that situation, the function must use recursion under a set of conditions that would avoid the possibility of an infinite loop. If a recursive call is done so that every call is to a simpler version of the problem, then the recursion can be made to stop when the problem has been simplified enough.

In this section, we look at some of the common problems that can be solved easily using recursion.

Sequence Operations

We often run into the needs to compute the sum or products of some sequence of formula. Suppose f(x) is the function of x, one may need to compute $\sum_{i=1}^{i=n} f(i)$ or $\prod_{i=1}^{i=n} f(i)$. The former function can be computed sequentially in the following pseudo-code logic:

```
answer = 0
for i in 1..n
 answer = answer + f(i)
```

The latter (product of the functions) is similar with multiplication instead of addition:

```
answer = 1
for i in 1..n
 answer = answer * f(i)
```

One can also write them as recursive functions which may be clearer in expressing the intent of the function:

```
function sum_sequence(int n):
 if (n == 0) return f(0)
  return f(n)+sum_sequence(n-1)
```

If we were to compute the time that it takes to run this recursive algorithm, we will end up that the time T(n) to compute sum_sequence(n) follows the relationship:

$T_n = T_{n-1} + c$, where c is a constant

Using induction, we can show that Tn will be O(n) in this case. More specifically, if $T_0 = d$ then $T_n = c.n+d$, which is O(n).

Permutation Generation

In some situations, we want to generate all the permutations possible with a sequence of items, e.g. generate all permutations of all letters in a word. When the number of items is variable, recursion is very useful in generating all permutations using a small amount of code.

The total possible number of permutations of a string with n distinct letter is n!. If some of the letters are repeated, e.g. let us say one letter occurs k times in a string which has length n, the possible number of permutations is n!/k!. If multiple letters repeat, the denominator would be the product of the factorials of the number of occurrences of each letter.

As an example, let us consider the word programmer. It consists of 10 letters with 3 occurrences of letter r and 2 occurrences of letter m. Its total number of permutation would be 10!/(2!.3!) = 302400. On the other hand, the word smile has 5 letters that are all unique. Its total number of permutations would be 5! or 120.

Enumerating all the possible permutations with recursion is relatively simple. The pseudo-code for generating all permutations of a list of distinct items can be given as:

```
function permute(word):
 if length of word is 1 then return a list containing word
 char1 = first character
 subword = word after removing first character
 sub_list = permute(subword)
 new_list = insert char1 in each location each word in sub_list
 answer = remove duplicates from new_list
 return answer
```

For this program, the running times follow the relationship $T_n = n.T_{n-1} + c$, where n is the length of the word being permuted. Using induction, one can show that T_n is O(n!).

Iterative Sequences

In mathematics, there are several classes of important numbers that are defined using an iterative sequence relationship. An iterative sequence relationship is one in which a sequence of numbers is defined. The definition of a next number in the sequence of numbers are defined in terms of the previous members of the sequence.

The most common among these types of sequence is the Fibonacci sequence which is defined iteratively as follows:

$$F_0 = 0$$

$$F_1 = 1$$
$$F_{n+1} = F_n + F_{n-1}$$

Each of the individual numbers F_i are known as Fibonacci numbers. The first few Fibonacci numbers are 0, 1, 1, 2, 3, 5, 8, 13, 21, 34 etc.

Fibonacci numbers are important for various applications in mathematics, computer science and biology. There were originally introduced to model the growth of rabbit population in a hypothetical context. However, they are not the only important category of numbers defined in an iterative manner. Other examples include the Lucas numbers which start with the same iterative relationship, except with different starting points. Defining L_i as the ith Lucas number, we get that:

$$L_0 = 2$$
$$L_1 = 1$$
$$L_{n+1} = L_n + L_{n-1}$$

The first few Lucas numbers will be 2, 1, 3, 4, 7, 11, 18, 29, 47, 76, 123,199…

Pell numbers are another sequence of numbers that are defined by the relationship:

$$P_0 = 0$$
$$P_1 = 1$$
$$P_{n+1} = 2P_n + P_{n-1}$$

The companion Pell numbers, or the Bell-Lucas numbers are defined by a similar relationship given by:

$$Q_0 = 2$$
$$Q_1 = 2$$
$$Q_{n+1} = 2Q_n + Q_{n-1}$$

Pell numbers have various applications in mathematics, e.g. an approximate value of $\sqrt{2}$ can be calculated as the value of $(P_{n-1}+P_n)/P_n$ for large values of n.

Recursion provides a convenient method for calculating these numbers. The code using recursion to calculate the different Fibonacci numbers would be:

```
function fibonacci(n):
    if n is 0 then return 0
    if n is 1 then return 1
    return fibonnaci(n-1)+fibonnaci(n-2)
```

The code for other numbers like Pell, Lucas and companion Pell can be calculated by writing similar type of code.

The code is simple, and its runtime is given by $T_n = T_{n-1} + T_{n-2}$. This however results in an exponential runtime since the solution to the runtime will be that T_n is a Fibonacci number. Using induction, one can provide that if F_n is the Fibonacci number, then $1.5^n < F_n < 2^n$. This is a very slow approach to computing the iterative sequence numbers.

The underlying cause for this poor performance of the approach is that each Fibonacci number gets computed multiple times. For example, if we were to compute F_5, it will compute F_4 and F_3, and then F_4 will also compute F_3. F_3 is being computed 2 times, and F_2 will be computed 4 times. The smaller Fibonacci numbers such as F^2 will get computed 2^n times when computing F_n.

In order to avoid this complexity, one approach would be to remember the sequences which were computed. We can initialize a global array of n capacity which would be initialized with -1 as the default value. When we need to compute Fn, we check if the kth entry in the global array is positive, and if so we can return the stored value. The revised code looks like the following:

```
global = array of N values initialized to -1
global[0] = 0
global[1] = 1

function fibonacci(n):
    if global[n] > 0 return global[n]
    global[n] = fibonnaci(n-1)+fibonnaci(n-2)
    return global[n]
```

This change allows one to compute the numbers in a linear amount of time since every number is computed only once. This approach also provides an approach in which time is being traded off against space – by keeping some global data structures, an algorithm can be made to perform better.

Recursion for Divide and Conquer

```
function bisection(a, b):
    if f(a).f(b) > 0 generate error
    c = (a + b)/2
    if absolute value of f(c) < threshold return c
    if f(a).f(c) < 0 return bisection(a,c)
    return bisection(c,b)
```

Divide and conquer is a useful strategy which works by reducing the problem to a smaller or simpler version that can be solved and then combines the results from the simpler problems as appropriate. Recursion provides a good approach to implement many divide and conquer algorithms.

Considering the problem of finding the root of an equation using bisection method, the recursive approach for finding the root would be as shown above assuming the threshold and function f are defined globally

In this particular case, the running time of the algorithm is O(log n) where n is the absolute value of (b-a).

Recursion for backtracking

Recursion is a great approach for solving many backtracking based algorithms. For the 8-queen problem, one can define a recursive solution which looks at the partial solution using the number or rows examined at the moment. The solution would look like the following:

```
function queens(soln, rows):
   if rows == 8 return soln
   for col in range of 0 through 7:
      tent_soln = add (rows+1, cols) to soln
      if viable(tent_soln):
            soln = queens(tent_soln, rows+1)
            if soln is not empty return soln
   // we have now tried all the columns placed
   Return empty_list
```

Many other games that require a backtracking based approach can also be solved easily using recursion.

Chapter Summary/Key Takeaways

In this chapter we looked at the use of recursion to solve some interesting problems in computer science. We also noticed how a judicious use of data structures such as arrays can result in a more efficient runtime for selected algorithms.

In the next chapter, we take a look at searching for data records.

Chapter 12. Search Algorithms

Searching for information is a common task that is needed in many different computer programs. The type of data structure that is used to enable the search can have a significant impact on the time it takes to search for an object.

To discuss searching tasks, we can make one of two assumptions – either assume that the data records that is in the data structure is unorganized or assume that the data records in the data structure are organized in a manner that enables rapid search. If the data is unorganized, then we have no recourse but to look at all the data records and see if one of them matches the item we are searching. The run-time complexity of this approach will always be O(n) regardless of the nature of data structure being used.

On the other hand, if we can organize the data records in a smart way, our searching approach can have better efficiency. However, we need to ensure that the organization of the data records remain valid even when new data records are added, or existing data records are deleted. Maintaining the organization may be complex when changes to data records are made.

In this chapter, we look at the task of organizing data within specific data structures and how that impacts the operation of adding, removing and searching for information. For ease of discussion, we will assume that all data records are integers. However, the same algorithms and approaches will be valid for any other data records as long as one can compare the data records to declare that one data record is smaller, equal or bigger than the other data record.

Another point worth repeating is that modern programming languages and operating systems come prepackaged with several searching algorithms. With GenAI, generating the code for searching through contents can be created very easily. The intent of this chapter is not to teach all the gory details of how searching can be optimized in implementation, but to provide the basic background with which a programmer can select among various searching options that are available to perform a task.

Searching in Arrays

For efficient searching in an array of integers, it is important that data in the array be maintained in a sorted manner. When the data is sorted, the first element could be either the smallest or the largest in the array. When the first element is the smallest, data is said to be sorted in the ascending order. When the first element is the largest, data is said to be sorted in the descending order. For ease of discussion, we will assume that data is always sorted in the ascending order.

In order to search for a specific search target, one can compare the target to the first and the last element in the array. If either of them matches, we are done. If the target is smaller than the first or larger than the last element, it does not exist in the array. Otherwise, we compare the target to the record that is in the middle of the array, i.e. at the location of (first+last)/2. If this matches, we are done. If the middle value is smaller than the target, we know that the target can only exist in the upper half of the array. If the middle value is larger than the target, we know that the target can only exist in the lower half of the array. We now perform the search recursively on the appropriate half.

This will sound like the divide and conquer scheme or the bisection scheme for finding roots of equations. The approach is very similar in principle, relying on halving the problem space repeatedly. The runtime for the search operation will be O(log n) for an array of size n.

In order for the search to be performed, data needs to be maintained in the ascending order even with addition or deletion of data records. If a data record is inserted, it can no longer be added to any arbitrary location. It must be inserted at the location which maintains the order. This search again can be done in O(log n) steps. However, when the new element is added, all elements that are larger than the new value being added needs to be shifted one step down. This results in an O(n) adjustments. This makes the addition of a new data record an O(n) operation.

The same holds true for removing objects. Since the searching process will not work if we are not able to compare the target to an empty location, we need to eliminate any gaps in the array when an object is removed. That shifting would require O(n) operations.

If we are operating in an environment where there are a lot of searches but relatively few updates (adds/removes) then maintaining information in a sorted array would be the appropriate choice. If we are operating in an environment where there are a lot of updates and searching is relatively infrequent, maintaining data in an unsorted array may be the more appropriate choice.

Searching in Lists

Lists do not permit direct access to any one of their entries other than the first or the last entry. This makes it hard to implement the searching tricks that relies on the content being sorted. On a standard list, search will be O(n), deletion will be O(n) since one needs to search for a target before deleting it, and addition can be made O(constant) by simply adding the object to the beginning or the end of the list.

If information needs to be maintained in a list for any reason, and searching is frequent, it may be worthwhile augmenting the list with an array that can maintain the information about the list records in a sorted manner. The list can maintain the information in any order, but the array maintains the information about the contents of the data records in the sorted manner.

Searching within Trees

Searching within the tree data structure requires maintaining data in the tree nodes in an order that permits easy access and retrieval through the tree by following only one of the branches down to the leaf. This requires arranging the data so that it enables easy comparison.

While there are many approaches that can use trees to improve the search process, let us consider a simple case where we will maintain the search information as a binary tree. We would also like the tree to be balanced so that the height of all leaves is the same, or at most with a difference of 1. The approach for data arrangement is for the data records for nodes in the left child subtree of a node to be smaller than the data record maintained at the node and for all nodes in the right subtree of any node to have values larger than that of the node. In this case, an in-order traversal of the tree would result in a sorted list of all node values.

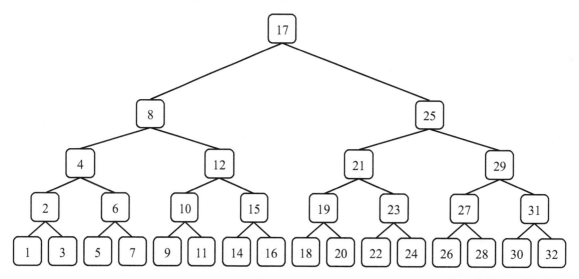

Figure 22. A balanced binary tree for efficient searching

An example of such a tree is shown in Figure 22. It has the numbers from 1-32 stored in the tree with missing number 13 in between. Searching for any number would require at most 4 links to be traversed in the tree.

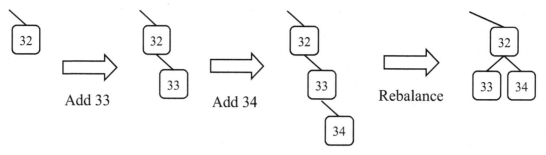

Leaf 34 has depth greater than leaf 30

Figure 23. Example of rebalancing of the tree on addition of a node

If we were to add the number 13 to the tree, it can be added as the left subtree of the node containing 14 and the desired properties of the tree would be maintained. However, consider the addition of nodes 33 and 34 in that order respectively. 33 will be added as the right child of 32, 34 will be added as the right child of 33. As shown in Figure 23, this creates a structure which does not maintain the properties of a balanced tree. In order to balance the tree, the linear segment of 32, 33

86

and 34 needs to be rebalanced making 33 be the parent of nodes 32 and 34. In general, additions and removals which occur on a tree would require rebalancing a subtree.

The rebalancing on addition and deletion is a complex procedure. Fortunately, existing software packages support efficient implementations of the rebalancing.

Searching with Maps

In a map or hash table, values are mapped to hash which corresponds to the index of the array in which the information is stored. Assuming the hash function does not result in a significant number of collisions, the map provides a theoretically O(constant) time for addition, deletion and searching. The effectiveness depends on the quality of the hash function.

Discussion

When designing the data structure to manage and maintain different types of information, we may need to select the appropriate data structure for managing and maintaining them. For this purpose, arrays and trees offer mechanisms to do a fast search when there are relatively few add/delete operations. Lists provide a more efficient mechanism when there are relatively more add/delete operations compared to the search operations. Hash tables provide a theoretically constant run-time for all operations for large amounts of data but require more complex operation when the hash function results in collisions.

At the current time, large data managed is done with database management packages. Nevertheless, need to manage data in software by creating a data structure may arise for other types of data in the program. If the data records being managed are small, managing them as arrays or lists may be more convenient despite their asymptotic poor performance on some type of operations. When larger amounts of data need to be managed, e.g. as an in-memory cache for an on-disk database, balanced trees and hash tables may be the preferred data structures to use.

Chapter Summary/Key Takeaways

In this chapter, we examined the issues of searching through a large volume of data, and the behavior of various data structures for this type of search.

In the next chapter, we take a look at searching for data records.

Chapter 13. Sorting Algorithms

Sorting algorithms are a staple component in the learning of data structure. There are many sorting algorithms. GenAI tools have made the implementation of most of the standard sorting algorithms relatively trivial. From a practical usage perspective, libraries that offer implementations of data structures provide their own sort functions. Therefore, the focus on this section is to look at a few sorting algorithms and understand their logic and behavior.

For all of the sorting algorithms in this chapter, we assume that the data consists of n integers placed into an array in some random order, and the objective is to sort them in an ascending order with the smallest integer first. We also assume that all of the integers in the array are unique. None of these assumptions can be relaxed without changing any of the observations about the various algorithms.

The Java code for all algorithms is available at https://github.com/dinesh-personal/data_structures/java/Chapter13.java.

Bubble Sort

The idea in bubble sort is to compare integers at adjacent positions in the array and swap them if the larger element is to the left. If one goes through the array once, the bubbling will move the largest element up one position. In order to ensure that all items and positions have been compared, one needs to make n passes through the array – if the array contains n integers. The pseudo-code for bubble sort would look like:

```
bubble_sort(array): // array has n items
   repeat for n times:
      for position p from beginning to one before last:
         if array[p] < array[p+1]then swap the elements
```

The big benefit of bubble sort is that it has a very easy code structure and provides a convenient routine if you need to write a sorting algorithm on your own data very quickly. The running time of bubble sort is $O(n^2)$

Selection Sort

```
selection_sort(array, start, end):
   if start == end then return // array has been sorted
   loc = location of smallest element between start and end
   swap elements at start position and loc
   selection_sort(array, start+1, end)
```

Selection sort makes n passes through the array. In the first pass it picks the smallest element in the array and puts in in the first place of the array. It repeats the process for the remaining element, the entire process being repeated n times. It can be expressed in the recursive manner as shown above with the initial call being `selection_sort(array, 0, n)`:

Finding the location of the smallest element can be done by going through the array once. A nested pair of loops provides a recursion-free implementation.

```
selection_sort(array, start, end):
   for i taking values from start to end:
      loc = location of smallest element between i and end
      swap elements at pos and loc
```

The running time of selection sort is $O(n^2)$

Insertion Sort

The idea in insertion sort is to make n passes through the array and at the end of the kth pass, ensure that any item to the left of the kth location is smaller than the item at the kth location. This effectively creates a sorted array till the kth location and at the end of nth pass, the entire array is sorted.

One way to do it is to find any element bigger than the element at the kth location which is in location between start and k, and then shift the element up by one place to make place for the element originally at the kth position to be inserted into the freed up slot.

The pseudocode looks like the following:

```
insertion_sort(array, start, end):
   for k taking values from start to end:
      key = element at location k
      counting j down from k-1;
         if array[j] > key then move array[j] to array[j+1]
      move k to the current value of j
```

The running time of insertion sort is $O(n^2)$

Merge Sort

Merge sort uses a recursive approach to sorting. It sorts the first half and the second half of the arrays and then combines the two sorted halves into a sorted list.

The recursive pseudo-code would be as follows:

```
merge_sort(array, start, end):
    if start >= end return empty array
    mid = start+end/2
    tmp_1 = merge_sort(array, start, mid)
    tmp_2 = merge_sort(array, mid+1,end)
    return merge_list(tmp_1, tmp_2)
```

Note that this pseudo-code is returning the array in contrast to the previous algorithms in which the pseudo-code was assuming that the arrays are being sorted in-place.

The merging of two sorted lists can be done by means of traversing each list and copying the smaller of the two into a merged list. If both the lists are sorted, this ensures that the combined elements have been merged into a sorted whole. This merging is $O(n)$.

The running time of merge sort will be given by the relation $T(n) = 2T(n/2) + O(n)$. The answer to this recursive relationship is $T(n) = O(n \log(n))$.

Quick Sort

Quick sort is another recursive algorithm but instead of dividing the arrays into half, it picks a pivot element. At each step of the recursion, the array is modified so that entries smaller than the pivot element to the left and larger than pivot element to the right. The benefit of this approach compared to merge sort is that the array can be modified in-place.

The pseudo-code which will now modify the array in place is as follows:

```
partition(array, start, end):
    pivot = array[end]
    boundary = start
    for pos from start to end:
      if array[pos] > pivot then:
          increment boundary and swap pos and boundary elements
    Increment boundary
    Swap last element with boundary element
    return boundary

quick_sort(array, start, end):
    if (start < end) return
    mid = partition(array, start, end)
    quick_sort(array, start, mid-1)
    quick_sort(array, mid,end)
```

Because of its ability to sort in-place, quick sort is often the preferred algorithm implemented in various libraries providing sorting capabilities.

Bucket Sort/Radix Sort

Bucket sort works by partitioning elements into multiple buckets, each bucket satisfying a set of conditions. These buckets can then be recursively sorted into smaller buckets if needed. As an example, let us consider a set of numbers. If we know that the numbers are all less than 100, we can partition them into 10 buckets of numbers from 1-9, 10-19, 20-19 … 90-99. A second tier of buckets can then sort these numbers into the precise order.

Radix sort is a variation of bucket sort which is designed primarily for strings. The strings are sorted into buckets belonging to the first character in the string, then for the second character in the string, and so on.

If the number of buckets are fixed, then bucket sort/radix sort can sort an array in $O(n)$ time. It also reduces the size of lists in each bucket which can then be sorted using one of the traditional sorting algorithms.

Chapter Summary/Key Takeaways

In this chapter, we examined various algorithms that can be used for sorting. While sorting functions are available in various libraries, sometimes a separate sorting algorithm is more convenient. Bubble sort, Selection sort and Insertion sort provide easy to write routines for sorting while quick sort and merge sort provide more efficient routines for sorting. When data can be put into discrete bins, bucket sort provide an efficient approach to sort data.

Chapter 14. Sample Exercise Problems

In this chapter, we present a few exercises for developing software programs that will use the knowledge of data structures and problem-solving techniques. For the solution of each of these problems, consider what type of abstractions ought to be defined to simplify the problem, and how those abstractions can be implemented using the data structures that you have learnt in this book.

Propositional Equivalence

Given a set of two propositions, can you figure out if they are equivalent. Consider for example the following two statements written using the syntax of Java programming language:

p || q

! (p && q)

These two statements are equivalent, i.e. they will always have the same truth value.

Given two statements consisting of various propositions, can you write a program to determine whether the two are equivalent? What abstractions will you define for this purpose? You can consider two variations, one in which the number of propositions is fixed (i.e. the statement consists of 4 propositions and operations among them), and one in which any number of variations can be present.

Limited Cryptoanalysis

Cryptoanalysis is the art of breaking secrets. In the chapter on arrays, you learnt about various approaches for obfuscation and encryption of messages. In this exercise, you are asked to put on a different hat, that of a law enforcement agency that must thwart evil people.

You are a good person working for law enforcement, and you have a colleague Linda who is also a good person. Linda can intercept and listen to some of the messages that are exchanged between Evan and Ethel, two evil persons. The scenario is as shown in Figure 24.

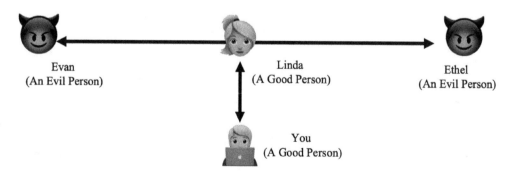

Figure 24. The scenario for cryptoanalysis

Linda has the following information about the evil people and what they send to each other:

1.   All messages they send is made up only of words from the following vocabulary:

PLOT, MEETING, RIOT, PLANNED, NEW YORK CITY, BOSTON, SAN FRANCISCO, WASHINGTON, MONDAY, TUESDAY, WEDNESDAY, THURSDAY, FRIDAY, SATURDAY, SUNDAY, ON, IN.

2.   All messages only use capital letters.

3.   All messages are encrypted by using a substitution cipher (Caesar's Cipher) in which each letter from 'A' to 'Z' are mapped one-on-one with another letter from 'A'-'Z'. Other letters are left unchanged.

4.   Each message takes the form of \<Evil Action\> \<Location\> \<Day\>.

The following is an example of a valid messages in plain text:

- RIOT PLANNED IN BOSTON ON SUNDAY

Linda only sees the coded message which has been encrypted using some key. You do not know the plain text or the key that is used for the encryption. You and Linda can only get access to the encrypted message. In other words, you and Linda may only see the following coded message when the first example is used.

- BAJH YSETTMQ AT CJXHJT JT XPTQEN

This uses a mapping key which has (R→ B, I →A, O→J, …). The mapping key is only partially listed.

Can you write a program which can output the plain-text messages from the encrypted message?

Note that since the vocabulary is limited, some of the techniques you may find for cryptoanalysis using GenAI systems may not work well. The limited vocabulary means that statistical distributions may not be valid, and you may not be right in assuming that the most common letter is E.

What are the abstractions you can define to solve this problem? What data structures will you use to manage the required information. Which information solving approach are you going to use?

To make the problem harder, consider two variations of this problem. In the first variation, you have the word boundaries, i.e. you see the following messages:

- BAJH YSETTMQ AT CJXHJT JT XPTQEN

In the other variation, you do not see the space intervals between the words, i.e. the message you get only has the following encrypted text:

- BAJHYSETTMQATCJXHJTJTXPTQEN

Without the spaces, the problem could be harder. Think of how you will define your abstractions and use one of the problem-solving approaches to address this challenges.

Crypto Arithmetic

Crypto Arithmetic or Verbal Arithmetic requires you to find the mapping between the digits 0-9 and the various letters in the alphabet which allow you to solve the following problems which make the expression valid mathematically. Some examples and their solutions are given below:

Problem	Solution	Explanation
TWO x TWO = THREE	T = 1, W = 0, O = 6, H = 3, R = 7, E =2	106 x 106 = 11236
SEND+MORE = MONEY	S=9, E=5, N=6, M=1, O=0, R=8, Y=2	9567+1085=10652
DO + RE = M I FA + SI=LA RE +SI + LA=SOL	D=5, O=4, R=3, E=7, M=1, I=9, F=2, A=0, S=6, L=8	54+37=91 20+63=83 37+63+83 =183

Can you write a program which will figure out the solution column given the problem column? Which abstraction will you define. Which data structures will you use? You can assume that only the addition and multiplication operators are used.

A Hero-Villain Game

This is a 2-dimensional board game which consists of a hero trying to fight his way through a series of villains. At each stage in the game, the hero faces one or more villains. The hero must pick a villain to fight with. If the hero fights the villain with a lower strength than his current strength, villain is defeated, other villains at that stage disappear, and the hero's strength increases by the strength of the defeated villain. The hero can now move on to the next stage of the game and face villains at the next stage. If the hero fights with a villain with a higher strength, the game ends with the death of the hero.

Let us consider the visual representation of the game shown in Figure 25, in which the hero (*Young Urchin*) has to reach and defeat the final villain – *The Emperor*. The hero picks the *soldider#2* in the first stage, gaining the strength of 175 at the next stage. Then he picks the *machine#3* gaining a strength of 325. Finally, he selects *Dark Lord* as the villain gaining a strength of 625 points – which allows him to defeat *The Emperor*.

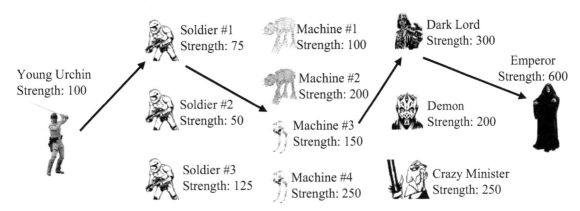

Figure 25. Illustration of a sample game

The game software needs to be provided with the initial strength of the hero, the name of the hero, and the names and strength of the villains at various stages. Assume that this input will be provided by means of a file which the game has to read in. You need to define the structure (i.e. the abstraction) defining the format of the input.

Can you use the game software to predict how many ways the hero can defeat the ultimate villain, i.e. the villain at the right-most side of the diagram? Can you use the game software to list the sequence of villains to overcome before defeating the ultimate villain? Can you do the same for a villain earlier in the game?

Predator-Prey System Simulation

A predator-prey system is an environment in which some predators and preys exist. The system tries to model the growth of predators and prey in an ecosystem. For this simulation, we can define some assumptions about how predators and prey evolve in the ecosystem. We can assume the system evolves through a discrete set of steps, one step per time with the following assumptions:

- Predators and preys are present in a 2-dimensional grid.

- Each cell can either be empty, contain a predator or contain a prey.

- At each time-epoch, a prey moves to a neighboring empty cell in the grid if it lets it get further away from a predator.

- At each time-epoch, a predator moves to a neighboring cell which contains a prey. It would eat the prey. If there are multiple such cells, it picks one randomly.

- At each time-epoch, if a predator does not have any neighboring cells with a prey, it moves randomly to one of the neighboring cells.

- If two predators end up moving to the same cell of the grid, only one survives

- At each timeframe, if an empty cell has two or more neighboring cells with a prey, a new prey is born in the empty cell.

- A predator which has not eaten a prey for Ktime-intervals dies off.

- The simulation starts with M predators and N preys in a SxS grid.

The program is modeled by the parameters of M, N, S and K. Can you write a program which will simulate 1000 instances and report in how many of these instances, the simulation results in all predators being led to extinction.

What type of abstractions can you define to approach the simulation? Which data structures are best suited for this simulation?

About the Author

Dinesh C. Verma is an IEEE Fellow, IBM Fellow, AAIA Fellow and Fellow of UK Royal Academy of Engineering. He has authored 11 books, 250+ technical papers and 250+ U.S. patents in the field of Computer Science.

He received his Ph.D. from University of California, Berkeley in 1992, B.Tech. in Computer Science from Indian Institute of Technology, Kanpur in 1987, and M.S. in Management of Technology from New York University Polytechnic in 1997. He has been an active researcher at IBM T.J. Watson Research Center since 1992.

In addition to his regular research work at IBM, Dinesh teaches Computer Science courses at various local colleges as an adjunct faculty. This book is the outcome from teaching data structure course at St. John's University in Queens.

www.ingramcontent.com/pod-product-compliance
Lightning Source LLC
LaVergne TN
LVHW080118070326
832902LV00015B/2654